Contents

Yogyakarta

A Cultural Cradle

At a hurried glance Yogyakarta looks like any town on the Indonesian island of Java. Unremarkable rows of small, neat houses and shops predominate. Like other towns on the island, a diverse assortment of vehicles, powered by an ingenious assortment of energy sources, everything from motors to oxen, crowd the dusty streets.

Closer inspection reveals some peculiarities, however. In one part of Yogyakarta, a small house with a roof at a rakish angle rears up on high stilts. Tucked behind it is a wooden cottage built like a gypsy caravan, complete with giant spoked wheels. Elsewhere, an entire neighborhood of ramshackle houses on a riverside is painted in garish graphics; art students squat on street corners, canvasses propped against a baroque lamp post as they paint the passing scene; a garbage truck announces itself, not with a klaxon, but with a loudspeaker mounted on the cab playing the clamorous musical accompaniment of a wayang puppet show. And in the parking lot of a hotel, an attendant, arms waving as he directs traffic, suddenly breaks into a few stylized dance movements.

No, Yogyakarta is not just another Indonesian town. Planted in the fertile heartland of Central Java, the cradle of the great Javanese empires, it is the center of Indonesia's grand cultural traditions, a city renowned for individual artistic expression, and the capital of ancient kingdoms, medieval empires and modern revolution. Yogyakarta today is an engaging melange of styles and moods, a cosmopolitan cultural melting pot.

In modern Yogyakarta, dynamic advances in art, theater and fashion counterpoint the frequent observances of ageless custom. The city boasts several theater groups, a large community of painters and sculptors, one of Indonesia's top universities and several other higher education institutions including two prestigious art schools.

The atmosphere of artistic creation, intellectual ferment and social experimentation complements the feeling that nothing at all

changes behind the walls of the *kraton*, the palace of the sultan of Yogyakarta. Despite the hundreds of tourists who pass through the courtyards and ornate pavilions each day, the two-century-old royal palace still functions much the same as in decades past.

The city's old and new personalities have at least one thing in common, though. A relaxed, unhurried pace pervades *kraton*, café and art school alike. That's how most Yogyanese

prefer to pass their days. The Javanese lifestyle emphasizes inner well-being and harmony over material acquisition or personal advancement, as is readily apparent to any traveler who ventures off any main road into any of the narrow alleyways that lead through the *kampung*, the incredibly cramped neighborhoods where most Yogyanese live.

A visitor to a Yogyakarta *kampung* need not have a specific goal in mind. In fact, it's better not to. Just walk aimlessly, *jalan-jalan* as the Indonesians say, without a guide. If appropriately well-mannered and apologetic, even a westerner can blunder anywhere short of entering a person's bedroom with-

Reflecting centuries of inbred dignity, a kraton *courtier pauses during a Garebeg ceremony (left).* Two wayang orang *performers take a break during dress rehearsal. In this form of* wayang, *human actors take the place of puppets (above).*

out causing offense or embarrassment. Just follow the narrow passageways through the *kampung*, smile and greet everyone pleasantly.

The ideal time for such a stroll is late afternoon, which the Yogyanese regard as the most pleasant time of day. The *kampung* is at its best. Fresh breezes chase away the midday heat and the warm light of the westering sun generates a halcyon atmosphere. Daily worries dissipate as the *kampung* residents occupy

of the Naga Tribe, Yogyakarta-born poet and playwright W.S. Rendra parodied the Javanese obsession for order by coining the resounding phrase "*Kerapihan untuk Pembangunan*," meaning "Tidiness for Development.

Along with this passion for order, the people of Yogyakarta display an impressive sense of etiquette. The Javanese look upon an uncouth person as "under-educated" and a rambunctious child is simply "not yet Javanese."

themselves with the small pleasures of tropical life. Passing food vendors proffer their wares, families relax on stools or benches in front of their houses eating *rojak*, *mie baso* and other tea-time snacks. Javanese gentlemen drink coffee, listen to the coo of their turtledoves and chat languidly with their friends. At sunset, the voice of the muezzin from the local mosque, amplified to distortion, calls out the time for prayer. A visitor to a *kampung*, quickly discovers that despite the overcrowding, the heat, the dust and lack of adequate sanitation, filth and squalor are noticeably absent. The most ramshackle homes are kept in meticulous order. In his play, *The Struggle*

Javanese military traditions still flourish during kraton ceremonies. Here, the captain of the guard stands with his troops during a Garebeg ceremony. During this festival animals are ceremoniously slaughtered and the meat distributed to the poor.

While walking through a *kampung*, an attempt to ask directions without prefacing the request with a polite "*Selamat Sore*" — "Good Afternoon" — will result in an answer; but it will carry with it a subtle, nonverbal reproof for such a lapse in manners. Of course, that answer may bear little relation to the questioner's intended destination. A Yogyanese would never consider brushing off a foreign guest's request for assistance with a brusque "*nggak tau*" — "don't know." To avoid being impolite, a Yogyanese will answer to the best of his ability, even if he is from another part of Java and disoriented himself. The solution when searching for a specific location in Yogyakarta is to ask three or four people, who will probably give widely varying directions, then follow a path determined by taking the trigonometric mean of all the answers.

The grace and utter civility of the Yogyanese is all the more remarkable considering their tempestuous history. Yogyakarta's role in the history of Java is similar to that of a character in an oddly-structured film. Like a lead actor who suddenly and inexplicably disappears from the screen while the story continues without him, Yogyakarta has for a few years or decades at a time been a superstar, then lapsed into somnolescence while history continued to run its relentless course elsewhere.

The valley between the Progo and Opak Rivers is among the most bountiful on earth. Routinely fertilized over the millennia by eruptions of volcanic lava and ash from nearby Mt. Merapi, the high agricultural yields gained with even rudimentary techniques guarantee a perennially large surplus of rice.

The giant Borobudur temple, which sits stolidly in the lush ricefields north of Yogyakarta, marks the area's first appearance in recorded history. Situated near the confluence of the Progo and a tributary, recalling the juncture of the holy Ganges and Jatna rivers in India, this Buddhist monument was originally intended to be a Hindu temple.

In AD 732, a Hindu noble named Sanjaya established a kingdom in the Progo-Opak valley that would later be called Mataram. In 775, he began the construction of a temple to commemorate his rule and the establishment of Hinduism on Java.

Ten years later, Mataram was suddenly in the hands of the Sailendra dynasty, a Buddhist family with links to the powerful Srivijaya kingdom in Sumatra. By this time, only the first two terraces of Borobudur were complete, and the walls uncarved. Perhaps deciding that the presence of King Sanjaya's Hindu

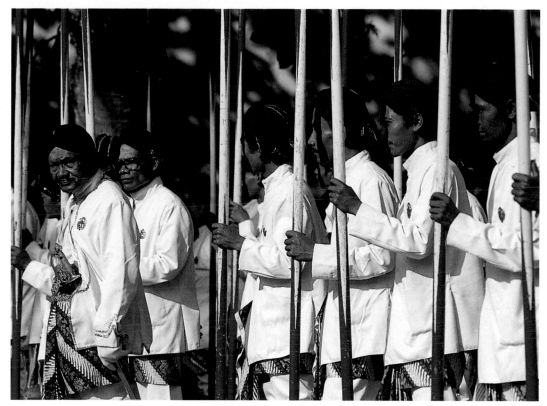

monument in the middle of their now-Buddhist kingdom was not in their best political interest, the Sailendra's adapted this initial stage to conform with Buddhist iconography and began a half century of more construction.

Consisting of two million cubic feet of rock wrapped around a small hill, Borobudur is the largest Buddhist stupa ever built and remains the largest man-made artifact in the Southern Hemisphere. An estimated 30,000 stonecutters and sculptors, aided by 15,000 carriers, labored for a half century on the 1.3 million stone blocks which make up the colossal sculptural monument. This astounding outlay of resources attested to the wealth and

Staff-bearing attendants march toward the Great Mosque during a Mutihan ceremony in their resplendent white clothes, immaculately groomed. The occasion is observed and celebrated amid much pomp and ritual.

15

fertility of ancient Central Java.

Borobudur was an early, and apparently successful, experiment in programmed instruction. As pilgrims approached the massive structure, they would be overwhelmed by its scale, making their minds sufficiently receptive to the teachings portrayed on the 1,500 relief panels.

Compelled by custom to follow a certain path around the five terraces of Borobudur, pilgrims viewed each panel in proper sequence. As the zig-zag corners prevented them from seeing more than a few steps ahead, their attention was focused on a few panels at a time, each graphically illustrating Buddha's biography and teachings. By the time a pilgrim reached the open upper terraces, he could fully appreciate the symbolism of the half-concealed Buddha statues, and the significance of the empty 10th terrace representing the ultimate nothingness of nirvana.

The declining power of the Sailendra's resulted in their defeat by a descendant of King Sanjaya, Rakai Pikatan. Apparently, the Sanjayas already had been ruling the outlying areas of Mataram as vassals of the Sailendras. Rakai Pakitan married a Sailendra princess and then overthrew that dynasty's incumbent rulers.

As the Sailendras fled to join their Srivijaya counterparts in Sumatra, power reverted to the Sanjayas. The Sanjayas rebuilt the main portals and made several other cosmetic changes to Borobudur, though with 500 statues of Buddha they could hardly convert it back to a Hindu temple. Nor did they want to. By then, the area's population was predominantly Buddhist. Instead of forcing Hinduism back on the people, the Sanjayas demonstrated a most Javanese trait, religious tolerance, by constructing two new Buddhist temples, Candi Sari and Candi Plaosan.

Rakai Pakitan went on to build his own monuments on the banks of the Opak. Whereas Borobudur is squat and solid, the Loro Jonggrang temple at Prambanan soars skyward to commemorate the resurgence of Hinduism in Mataram.

In contrast to the moral didacticism of Borobudur, Loro Jonggrang, is dedicated to Siva, the God of Destruction, in a celebration of Hindu literature and aesthetic values.

Courtiers take their official duties seriously, comporting themselves with grave dignity during the long ceremonies. The elaborate protocol where old fashioned ideals of courtesy and etiquette were practiced in the old days are still being observed today.

Sultan Hamengkubuwono VII sits in state on his throne in the Siti Hinggi. His costume includes a batik sarong decorated with the parang rusak barong pattern, indicating his royal status. His jacket is imprinted with fine gold leaf.

Historical Chronology

732 — The area of Yogyakarta first appears in recorded history when Sanjaya, a Hindu noble, establishes territorial rule in the Mataram region. The earliest temples built in central Java date from this period, including the foundation of the great Borobudur temple.

750 — The Buddhist Sailendra dynasty overthrows Sanjaya. They adapt the initial Hindu stages of Borobudur to Buddhism and, during the next half century, create the world's largest Buddhist monument. The Sailendra kings also build the neighboring temples of Pawon and Mendut, and the Kalasan and Sewu temple groups near the Opak River.

856 — Rakai Pikatan, a descendant of King Sanjaya, overthrows the Sailendra dynasty. The return of Hinduism to Mataram sparks a new spate of temple building, most notably the Prambanan complex near the Opak River.

930 — A generation after the completion of Prambanan, Mataram temporarily vanishes from history when the reigning king, Sindok, moves his court to the Brantas Valley near Surabaya. The move to East Java has never been explained. Some experts believe a devastating eruption of Mt. Merapi, or an epidemic may have caused it. Whatever the reason, most of the population probably moved with King Sindok.

1400 — The Hindu empire of Majapahit, founded by the descendants of the Sanjaya Dynasty and centered in Trowulan, East Java, controls or influences much of the Indonesian archipelago. The trading towns on Java's north coast begin their conversion to Islam, a new religion brought from Arabia by way of India.

1512 — The first Europeans other than individual travelers, a four-ship Portuguese merchant fleet, arrives in Indonesian waters. For the next 150 years, the Europeans confine their activities to the coasts, leaving the Javanese interior to work out its own destiny.

1550 — A nondescript Hindu state, Pengging, is conquered by an adventurous coastal Javanese noble, Sunan Kudus. The resulting new state, Pajang, centered near present day Kartasura, heralds the resurgence of the resilient Mataram dynastic line.

1570 — Kyai Gedhe Panamaham, reputed to be a direct descendant of the Majapahit kings and through them the ancient Mataram rulers, establishes a power center near present-day Yogyakarta as ancient Mataram becomes repopulated. Largely deserted for six centuries, the old empire's rich lands return to history.

1587 — Senopati, the son of Kyai Gedhe, conquers the Kingdom of Pajang. He moves the all-important pusaka, the holy regalia of kings to his court in Kota Gede. Senopati is a historical figure whose life spawns many legends and myths. He is regarded as the first king of the second, or modern, Mataram Empire.

1596 — The first shipload of Dutchmen to reach the East Indies, led by Admiral Cornelius van Houtman, stumbles ashore at Banten in western Java after a voyage fraught with disease and dissension. Returning to Holland with a light load of spices and a third of the crew, the small profit realized by the expedition spurs the Dutch mercantile advance into the East Indies. All commerce is soon organized under one of the world's first trading cartels, the Netherlands East India Company, also known as the VOC.

1601 — Senopati dies and his son Penembahan Krapyak consolidates the new state, defeating a rebellious relative in Demak and severely weakening Mataram's greatest rival, the Kingdom of Surabaya. In a move equally important in Javanese eyes, Krapyak constructs a more formidable kraton in Kota Gede, and encourages the development of literature and the arts. These activities serve to legitimize the court which is now much more than an upstart conqueror.

1613 — Krapyak's son, Agung, begins a campaign to unite all of Java under his rule. In a string of military victories he subdues rebellious Pajang, further weakening Surabaya. However, Agung underestimates the power of the Europeans.

1619 — A VOC force under Jan Pieterszoon Coen crosses Agung's self-declared boundary by taking the north coast trading town of Jayakarta, for the first time carving out a piece of Javanese soil for the Europeans.

1625 — After years of war, Agung finally conquers Surabaya.

1628 — Agung's attempt to block the Europeans fails, a major setback. The first siege of Batavia lasting five months meets with stinging defeat.

1629 — A subsequent one-month siege of Jakarta is an unqualified disaster. The Dutch fight off one attack by dumping freshly-filled latrine buckets over the walls onto the attackers. Their reaction is noted by the first recorded journalistic quote in the Malay language: *"Shaitan Belanda itu berkalay dengan tay"* which frankly translated means, "Those Dutch devils fight with shit." Beset by disease and starvation, the Javanese army limps home from Batavia. The Dutch remain firmly entrenched in their seaside fortress, poised to become the dominant force in Javanese politics for the next 300 years.

1640 — Agung ejects the Balinese from eastern Java, consolidating Mataram's control over the eastern two-thirds of the island. That year, with the approval of Mecca, he takes the title "sultan."

1646 — Sultan Agung dies and is buried at Imogiri. His son takes the imperial title *susuhunan* and the name Amangkurat I. He moves his court to Plered, near Yogyakarta and constructs a brick *kraton* to signify the solidity of new Mataram.

1648 — Amangukurat I alienates most of his powerful subordinate nobles and officials with new policies designed to centralize economic and political power for royal benefit. Then he attempts to deter the threat of rebellion by slaughtering all of his potential opponents, as many as 6,000 people by some estimates.

1670 — The crown prince, who detests his father as much as anyone, conspires with Trunojoyo, another disaffected noble. Earlier, Trunojoyo had fled to Madura and raised an army of fierce Madurans and Makassarese pirates forced from their homeland in the southern part of the island the Dutch call Celebes, now known as Sulawesi.

1672 — An eruption of Mt. Merapi, an out-of-season monsoon, an earthquake and a lunar eclipse occur, mystical portents that leave no doubt that great change was imminent in Java. Moreover, the new Javanese century approaches. The 17th century on the Javanese calendar is to commence in March, 1677, when the Javanese believe that the current cycle will soon be complete and the empire will fall.

1675 — As if on cue, Trunojoyo's forces rampage through Java and Sultan Agung's fragile empire collapses with hardly a fight. Many regional Javanese nobles now join the rebellion.

1677 — Trunojoyo captures Plered, sending the king and crown prince fleeing. By this time, the crown prince harbors no illusions that Trunojoyo will cooperate further with him. Trunojoyo returns to Surabaya with his prized booty, the Mataram royal treasury.

1679 — VOC troops march against Surabaya and capture Trunojoyo, delivering him to Amangkurat II to be personally stabbed to death. As the VOC troops defeat the rebel forces, most Javanese nobles declare allegiance to the new king.

1680 — Amangkurat II establishes his court in Kartasura, near the capital of the Pajang kingdom conquered by Senopati. His brother, Puger, attacks Kartasura on two occasions, but is repelled by the VOC both times.

1681 — Having failed to overthrow Amangkurat II, Puger recognizes the authority of the Kartasura ruler.

1686 — Amangkurat II plots with Surapati, a Balinese slave turned adventurer wanted by the Dutch. Francois Tack, the new VOC ambassador to Kartasura, arrives with his troops to take up his position to capture Surapati. Amangkurat II pretends to assault Surapati's army and draws the Dutch into an ambush. Tack and 73 Dutch troops are murdered. Later, the Dutch discover correspondence between Amangkurat II to various freebooters and to all regional powers, including the English East India Company, proposing common cause against the Dutch. The VOC rapidly loses trust in the Kartasura court.

1703 — Amangkurat II dies, and is succeeded by his son, Amangkurat III. Puger flees from the court and tries to persuade the Dutch that he is the rightful heir.

1704 — Believing Puger's claims, the Dutch declare him Susuhanan Pakubuono I. Amangkurat III, justifiably annoyed, starts the first of three succession wars in 18th-century Java. But he is defeated and exiled to Ceylon (present-day Sri Lanka).

1719 — The death of Pakubuono I results in a second war of succession. Pakubuono I's successor, his son Amangkurat IV, attempts with little success to rule under the chaotic conditions of Mataram, and dies in 1726 of suspected poisoning. He is succeeded by his son, Pakubuono II, who promptly embarks on the most catastrophic reign in modern Javanese history.

1740 — Events in distant Batavia again have great impact on Mataram. Growing tensions between Dutch residents of Batavia and the ethnic Chinese result in a massacre of more than 10,000 Chinese in Tanah Abang, just outside the city walls. A small army of Chinese flee Batavia and rampage along the north coast attacking Dutch installations. Pakubuono II sends troops to assist the Chinese. When the Chinese are defeated, he immediately begs and receives forgiveness from the Dutch. The rebel princes and the Chinese are down, but not out. Now that the *kraton* is pro-Dutch, insurrectionist forces are soon at the palace gates. It falls to them in 1742. The fleeing susuhunan heads right for the Dutch, who defeats the rebels and restores a grateful Pakubuono II to the throne.

1745 — The battered and unlucky Kartasura Kraton is moved to Surakarta, 12 kilometers to the northeast, in a great royal procession led by Pakubuono II dressed as a bridegroom. Gamelans play, ministers march and armies of attendants carry great boxes filled with the holy regalia of the *kraton*. Everything belonging to the court is transplanted, including the sacred banyan trees and the king's pet lion.

1746 — Pakubuono II offers a deal to his sometime rebel half-brother, Mangkubumi. In exchange for driving the rebel princes from nearby Sukabumi (now called Sragen) Mangkubumi would be granted control over 3,000 households. Mangkubumi accepts the deal and crushes the rebels. But when he returns to Kartasura, Pakubuono II reneges on his promise, openly humiliating Mangkubumi for being overly ambitious. Mangkubumi then joins forces with a rebel prince, Mas Said, in the third and final war of succession. The two armies romp through central Java, massacre a company of Dutch soldiers, and attack Surakarta itself.

1749 — When Pakubuono II dies and his son mounts the throne as Pakubuono III, Prince Mangkubumi simultaneously declares himself the third Pakubuono and establishes a court in the village of Yogya, near the original Mataram courts of the previous century. With the majority of Javanese backing his claim, the Dutch cannot afford to ignore Mangkubumi. The Dutch and Mangkubumi agree to divide Mataram into two equal kingdoms. Pakubuono III is not consulted on the matter.

1755 — Pakubuono III and Mangkubumi sign the Treaty of Gijanti, dividing Mataram into the Susuhunate of Surakarta and the Sultanate of Yogyakarta.

1792 — Mangkubumi dies and is succeeded by the crown prince, who becomes Hamengkubuwono II. He replaces his father's able advisors with court lackeys and institutes oppressive taxation and forced labor.

1799 — Reeling under the combined blows of a decline in the spice trade, the mounting burdens of their military presence in Java, and widespread corruption and inefficiency, the Dutch East India Company's resources are strained to the breaking point. On the last day of the 18th century, the VOC declares bankruptcy. All of its assets are taken over by the Dutch government.

1808 — King Louis of Holland, Napoleon's brother, appoints Marshall Herman Willem Daendels as governor-general in Batavia. Daendels proves to be a staunch revolutionary, who attempts not only to correct the European administrative abuses, but to curtail the feudal powers of the Javanese nobles

1810 — In the wake of a local rebellion by a Yogyakarta court official, Daendels demands changes in court protocol, and an apology. Hamengkubuwono II bristles and refuses outright. Daendels marches on Yogyakarta and deposes Hamengkubuwono II in favor of his son, who becomes Hamengkubuwono III.

1811 — The political events of faraway Europe again touch Java when the British conquer the Far Eastern possessions of French-dominated Holland. Hamengkubuwono II takes advantage of the confusion to remount the throne. But he proves no less hostile to the British than to their predecessors. Thomas Stamford Raffles, as reformist-minded as Daendels but more reasonable and diplomatic, assumes control of Java for the British. However, diplomacy proves of little use against the arrogant Hamengkubuwono II. Raffles meets Hamengkubuwono II in late 1811, an occasion which almost leads to armed combat in a crowded room.

1812 — Learning of secret correspondence between Yogyakarta and Surakarta to join forces and oust the British, Raffles marches on the Yogyakarta *kraton* with the help of the crown prince and Hamengkubuwono II's brother Natakusuma. Scaling the massive ramparts, Raffles' troops loot the library, archives and treasury, humiliating the Javanese. Hamengkubuwono II is exiled to Penang, and his son is once more installed as Sultan. As a reward for his assistance, the British set up a subsidiary princedom in Yogyakarta, giving Natakusama control of 4000 households and the royal title Paku Alam I.

1816 — The Dutch regain their East Indies colony when Napoleon's wars of conquest in Europe and Russia are curtailed.

1825 — In an attempt to oust the Europeans from Java, Prince Diponegoro begins five years of guerrilla insurrection, the Java War. Though Diponegoro initially enjoys great popular support and notches up a string of victories, most Javanese nobles prudently side with the Dutch.

1827 — In an ironic move, the aged and still implacably hostile Hamengkubuwono II is plucked from exile and returned to the throne, but with no effect.

1830 — With the Java War winding down, Diponegoro is lured into negotiation, captured instead and exiled to Sulawesi. The Yogyakarta Kraton loses the last vestiges of political power.

1840 — The *kraton* library, looted by the British in 1812, is restocked as the sultan and his court patronize literary activity. Paku Alam II and Paku Alam III are authors themselves, and do much to promote modern Javanese literature.

1851 — Raden Saleh, a Javanese aristocrat who spent 20 years in Europe studying under Delacroix and becoming a well known court painter, returns to Java to paint at the Yogyakarta Kraton. This is the beginning of western art in Yogyakarta.

1860 — As European style gilt chairs, Italian marble, crystal chandeliers and Dutch military uniforms and decorations appear, the splendor of the Yogyakarta Kraton reaches new heights. The prestige of the court remains high among the masses.

1890 — When Dutch abuses in the colony are publicized, pressure from Holland forces the Batavia government to abolish many of the oppressive burdens on the Javanese, and to grant them greater educational and business opportunities. This policy would again backfire on the Dutch. Some Indonesians, especially those with comfortable positions as liaison officials between the Dutch administrators and colonized peoples, use the new opportunities to become ersatz Dutchmen. But a significant number band together to employ their newly-acquired knowledge and sophistication for their own ends.

1896 — The Dutch present eight cartloads of relief

panels and statues from the Borobudur to visiting King Chulalongkorn of Siam (now Thailand). The Dutch come to regard Borobudur as a limitless supply of garden ornamentation. They adorn thousands of colonial gardens with priceless statues plundered from the monument. A few years later, Borobudur suffers the ultimate indignity of having a teahouse built on the tenth level, which represents nirvana.

1908 — The first nationalist organization, *Budi Utomo,* founded as an association of Javanese medical students, holds its inaugural congress in Yogyakarta. Other such organizations spring up during the next decade, many based in Yogyakarta. Not all draw their support from the local intelligentsia. The Subjects of Yogyakarta, a group of peasants led by Prince Surjodiningrat, embarrasses the other nationalist groups by easily obtaining mass support.

1930s — The Yogyakarta court devotes most of its energy to a game of cultural one-upmanship with the rival Surakarta Kraton. Hundreds of dancers and other artists fill the *kraton* pavilions in spectacular performances. Meanwhile the colonial administration clamps down on the nationalist organizations by banning meetings and imprisoning leaders. In turn, the groups become more strident and less willing to compromise.

1939 — The crown prince is recalled from school in the Netherlands by the ailing Hamengkubuwono VIII. When he passes away in September, the crown prince mounts the throne as Sultan Hamengkubuwono IX.

1942 — The Japanese sweep through Southeast Asia. Although the Japanese troops are initially greeted as liberators from the Dutch colonial masters, it soon becomes apparent that these new overlords are more cruel and oppressive than their predecessors. All of the archipelago's resources are shipped overseas as the Japanese combine the East Indies with the other conquered Southeast Asian nations into the Greater East Asia Co-Prosperity

Sphere, an "organization of equals" in which Japan is more equal than all the other member countries combined.

1942-1945 — The Japanese Occupation, though a great hardship, proves to be a golden opportunity for Indonesian nationalism. When the Japanese intern the Dutch nationals, the educated nationalists are placed in positions of bureaucratic responsibility previously denied them. During the next three years, the Javanese elite gain self-confidence while the nationalist leaders prepare the groundwork for independence when the Japanese pull out.

1945 — Indonesia declares itself an independent nation on August 17, two days after the Japanese surrender. In September, the British land in Java as interim administrators until the Dutch can return to reestablish their government. To their consternation, the British are branded as interlopers invading a sovereign nation. In spite of the assassination of British General Mallaby in Surabaya, the British forces attempt to muddle through the situation with diplomacy and tact.

1946 — The Dutch return and attempt to recolonize the islands. When they occupy Batavia in January, the Republican Government moves to Yogyakarta, which remains the capital of the Indonesian Republic until 1950.

1947 — In June, Republican pilots, flying reconditioned Japanese byplanes, bomb Dutch positions in Ambarrawa and Semarang. In retaliation, Dutch fighters shoot down an unarmed DC-3 flying Red Cross medical supplies into Yogyakarta. The Dutch suffer a major setback in world opinion.

1948 — The Dutch capture and occupy Yogyakarta on December 18. Retreating to the hills, guerrilla forces commanded by General Sudirman harass Dutch troops for months and at one point even retake Yogyakarta for six hours. The Republicans have no hope of defeating the Dutch militarily, but world opinion comes to their aid. General disapproval in the United Nations and the embarrassing disclosure that most of Holland's Marshall Plan reconstruction funds are being used to support the occupying army in the East Indies lead to demands for a settlement.

1949 — The Republican Government returns to Yogyakarta on July 6. On December 27 the Dutch formally transfer sovereignty of the archipelago, except for West Irian, to the Indonesians. The nation's first president, Sukarno, moves the government to Jakarta on December 27.

1950 — Life in Java returns to some semblance of normalcy after eight years of war and revolution. Essential goods, however, are still in short supply as attempts to reconstruct Indonesia's ravaged economy falter under a succession of unstable governments.

1953 — The reconstruction of the Loro Jonggrang temple at Prambanan is completed. At the same time, it becomes evident that Borobudur is collapsing under its own weight as rain seeping through cracks in the uncovered monument erodes the soft soil underneath.

1956 — The Communist-dominated People's Cultural Institute (LEKRA) determines permissible standards and subject matter in art. Consequently, many Yogyanese artists are suppressed, others join the communists and sacrifice art to social realism, while some simply leave the country.

1962 — The first Sendratari, a combination of art, drama, and dance, is held in Yogyakarta, supposedly in connection with a tour group. Created by Bagong Kussudiardja and other dancers, Sendratari combines traditional wayang wong with western ballet techniques. Now, Sendratari is performed at Prambanan during the four nights of the full moon during the dry season.

1965 — The growing communist party, the PKI, attempts a coup. It is quickly put down by a rising general named Suharto and many communist leaders go into hiding in Yogyakarta and other parts of central Java.

1966 — Suharto restores order to the country and designates Jakarta as Indonesia's official capital, leaving Yogyakarta to resume its longtime role as Java's cultural capital.

1967 — Sukarno is relieved of his presidential powers. Professor Soekmono, Head of the Indonesian Archaeological Institute, appeals to delegates of the International Congress of Orientalists for help in saving Borobudur. The Indian delegates propose that UNESCO coordinate the operation. Funds are raised, and the project officially commences in 1973.

1968 — Acting President Suharto is officially confirmed as the new leader of the Republic. He appoints Yogyakarta Sultan Hamengkubuwono IX as vice president.

1974 — Sultan Hamengkubuwono IX gives away four of his daughters in a mass royal wedding ceremony. This event was much less spectacular than a similar ceremony in the 1930s, because the Sultan wishes to set an example of austerity.

1983 — After ten years of restoration costing US$60 million, Borobudur is reopened as Yogyakarta's centerpiece tourist attraction.

1985 — Another restoration program begins at Loro Jonggrang temple at Prambanan. The project later includes the outer temples in the complex.

1988 — Hamengkubuwono IX, Indonesia's last official sultan, dies. He plays a pivotal role in the revolutionary struggle against the Dutch.

1989 — Crown prince Mangkubumi ascends the throne as Hamengkubuwono X.

The Venerable Old Garuda

Although Indonesia lacks an internationally-renowned grand colonial hotel such as Singapore's Raffles or Bangkok's Oriental, Yogyakarta's Hotel Garuda has recently recreated some measure of the early years of Dutch colonial elegance.

The venerable hotel, largely neglected since independence, has been totally renovated. Once again the Garuda reigns as Yogyakarta's premier accommodation and its rich history gives it an appealing character.

There is nothing particularly notable about an average room at the Garuda. And the service is standard Javanese — adequate, with endless smiles and all around good nature making up for frequent lapses.

But in an untypical moment of inspiration and taste, the restoration managed to retain much of the colonial style and atmosphere, including stained-glass windows, Dutch-style double doors and outside sitting areas in the major suites. Even Director-General of Tourism Joop Ave, whose uncompromising sense of artistic style is well-known, praised the hotel when it reopened.

Built in 1911 and pretentiously named Grand Hotel de Djogja (the old Dutch spelling of the city's name), the hotel consisted of small cottages flanking the central structure. In 1932, the two double-story wings that stand today replaced the cottages. The original central building was also retained.

The hotel's first decades were idyllic. The transplanted European elegance of the Grand Hotel de Djogja reflected the leisurely lifestyle of the plantation administrators, government officials, and adventurous travelers who used the hotel.

The end of that era came in 1942, when the Grand Hotel de Djogja received its first uninvited guests — the Imperial Japanese occupying forces.

Renamed Hotel Asahi, the Dutch managers were imprisoned and replaced by three Japanese: Kawasaki, Suzuki, and Yamana. Ironically, their names came within a single consonant of foreshadowing the motorized Japanese vanguard that has taken over the streets of Yogyakarta forty years later.

After the Japanese defeat in 1945, the name, management and clientele of the hotel changed again. The Hotel Asahi became the Hotel Merdeka, the Freedom Hotel. In January 1946, the Hotel Merdeka became the home and office of several Revolutionary Government ministers when President Sukarno moved the capital of the brand new Republic of Indonesia from beleaguered Jakarta to somewhat safer Yogyakarta.

Yogyakarta was not much of an improvement, however. The city's resources were quickly overburdened by the influx of Republican soldiers and refugees. But even as supplies dried up during the Dutch blockade, the Hotel Merdeka maintained reasonable service, rivaling the British talent for preserving standards in the midst of adversity.

"Even during periods when we could only offer canned food, we kept to our standards," said Sugiyono Joyodiharjo, who was the general manager at the time. "It was easier when the United Nations Good Offices Committee stayed at the hotel, because they had their food airdropped to them, and they shared it with us." General Sudirman, the ranking general of the Revolutionary Army, stayed for months in the Hotel Merdeka,

Though now dominated by a seven-story concrete edifice designed to accommodate large tour groups, the original wings of the Garuda Hotel have managed to retain their colonial charm and elegance which gives the hotel much of its appeal.

fighting the new Republic's hunger, privation, and his own tuberculosis.

The hotel even spawned a Javanese-style romance. Admiral Subyatito used a young room boy, Sutrisno Sukowati, as a go-between to carry courtship letters to his future wife, the sister-in-law of Vice President Mohammed Hatta.

When the Dutch invaded Yogyakarta in 1948 and commandeered the hotel, over half of the employees resigned. Even General Manager Sugiyono left to open a food stall in the market.

Those employees who remained to work for the

Dutch were literally trapped in the building. To walk the streets would invite being gunned down by a guerrilla sniper.

When the Dutch withdrew for good in 1950, the government returned to Jakarta and the hotel was renamed the Garuda, after the mythical eagle that is Indonesia's national symbol. In 1975 the government gave the hotel to Natour, a government-owned hotel chain. Today the hotel offers resonable facilities at a reasonable price, and the advantage of being located smack in the heart of fascinating Jalan Malioboro.

The temples scattered around the environs of Yogyakarta are the only tangible remains of the ancient Mataram kingdoms. Because of the paucity of other historical evidence, accounts of wars or other great historical events of that time are strictly conjecture.

It is likely that the population of Mataram did little else but grow rice and construct great monuments during the Sailendra and Sanjaya

their empires, the early kings had to convince the populace of their right to govern. They imported religious scholars from India — Indonesia's first foreign consultants — to encourage and disseminate the Indian religions which gave the king important status as the semi-divine representative of God on earth.

Furthermore, by involving the populace in the construction of religious monuments, each subject might feel he had a share in the

dynasties. Certainly the projects, all completed in just over a century, would have taxed the region's resources and exhausted its manpower. In sharp contrast to today, Java was underpopulated until the 19th century and had large tracts of wilderness and virgin rain forest. The relatively small population living along the Progo and Opak rivers, who formed the monument-building workforce, would have had to invest most of their time and energy to construction. This might have been the precise intention of the Mataram kings. The animist societies of early Java had no place for a monarch; leadership began and ended at the clan or village level. In building

Islam in Java takes many forms, from devout fundamentalism to a mixture of Islam, Hinduism and animism. But whatever form it takes they all share the same basic characteristics — gentleness and a high degree of tolerance.

glory of Hinduism and Buddhism, and, by extension, the glory of the king. Through the artistic talents of their stonecutters and the backbreaking work of the common man, the Mataram kings sought to reinforce their legitimacy and to propagate their authority for eternity.

Nevertheless, the temple building program did not have the intended result. By AD 930, a generation after the completion of Prambanan, the ancient Mataram kingdom mysteriously disappeared from history. The power center moved to the Brantas Valley near Surabaya in East Java. The cause of this sudden migration remains unknown. Some theories attribute it to a devastating eruption of Mt. Merapi that covered the entire region in volcanic debris. The recent excavation of the perfectly-preserved Sambasari temple from under three meters of ash supports this theory. The temple, which dates from this period,

shows no sign of damage by looters.

Whatever the reason, most of Mataram's population dispersed, and Mataram disappeared from history. Those who remained in Mataram lived quietly in the shadow of Mt. Merapi for a half millennium, unbothered by glory-hunting kings. If they built any more temples, they were of wood, similar to those illustrated on the reliefs of Borobudur, and have long since vanished. Whether these tem-

O ne system of beliefs shared by most Yogyanese is a form of ancestor worship. This is not necessarily a worship of their own grandfathers, but a faith in the mystic power of the illustrious founders of the Mataram Empire.

In fact, at 8 p.m. on any Thursday night, a large crowd forms in front of a graveyard in Kota Gede, a village five kilometers south of Yogyakarta. Dressed in traditional Javanese

ples were Hindu or Buddhist, no one knows and it doesn't really matter. After the move to East Java, the people adopted elements from both religions and Hinduism and Buddhism lost their distinct identities.

During the 13th to 15th centuries the East Java rulers called themselves Hindu-Buddhist. When Islam was introduced in the 15th century, the rapid acceptance of this third new religion was less a conversion than another adaptation. The tenets of Islam were superimposed over the older Hindu-Buddhist religion which in turn had been overlaid on the ancient animist beliefs. A modern Javanese could therefore describe himself as a Buddhist Muslim, or Christian Hindu, or virtually any combination of the three. The supple Javanese mind simply accepts the valid attitudes, doctrines and ideas from whatever religion, and discards the rest.

costumes and carrying candles which cast dancing shadows over the high looming walls, the supplicants pray and meditate, seeking to tap the mystic power of the ancestors whose remains rest inside.

Supplicants gather around a small pool beside one wall, filling small vials with the rainwater that has drained from the graveyard. They believe contact with the tombstones within has sanctified the water.

About 80 princes and other nobles of Yogyakarta and the royal house in neighboring Surakarta are buried here. But the primary object of the supplicants' attention is the tomb of Senopati, a 16th century military ruler. A

An archetype of grace, Yogyakarta's court dancers practice in a quiet corner of the kraton. *Though court performances are now a shadow of the extravaganza's mounted during the 1930s, classical artistic traditions still flourish inside the* kraton *walls.*

A court dancer (right) performs the Tari Golek, a dance based on the movements of three-dimensional wayang golek puppets. Classical dance is a major component of every Javanese girl's education (**below**) and requires years of arduous training.

Dancing through Life

T he natural rhythm of the people of Java complements the island's lush, lyrical landscape. Their lithe figures move gracefully through a terraced paddy field, bobbing down a path bearing bottles on their backs or sheaves of rice on their shoulders as if swaying to some inaudible songs in the wind.

Such mesmerizing movement long ago rippled through Java's rich culture. Bas-relief panels on temples as old as the Borobudur and Prambanan depict various forms of classical dance. But it wasn't until the 19th century, when the courts had little else to do but devote themselves to cultural pursuits, that dance became a primary art form. The Yogyakarta kraton supported a substantial troupe and made a great effort to develop and refine the existing forms.

In the process, dance became stylized and abstract. Teachers placed more emphasis on technique and precision than vitality. In the Serimpi, a court dance traditionally performed by princesses, the dancers at times seemed motionless, even though they acted out a vigorous tale of war between rival fighters.

By custom, the court forbid some of these dances from being seen by outsiders and commoners, including the Bedoyo, which is no longer performed in Yogyakarta and only staged once a year in Solo. It celebrates the reunion of Loro Kidul with Senopati. Legend has it that Loro Kidul herself attended the

Bedoyo performances, and after the show "married" the presiding sultan.

It takes patience and a particular attitude to fully appreciate the ceremonial nature of the classical dances of Yogyakarta. They are almost meditative in quality. They represent and celebrate the virtues of Javanese culture: grace, elegance, and inner peace.

Dance was also used to educate Javanese children especially girls, in priyayi (official) values. Dance taught them poise, modesty and the awesome degree of self-control that is the most desired character trait of a cultured Javanese.

For foreigners, the dance traditions of Yogyakarta make for interesting anthropology but less than rousing entertainment for all but those in the mellowest mood. The traditional court dances for the most part remain inaccessible to most Westerners and, for that matter, to many of the Javanese themselves.

Nevertheless, in the cultural melting pot of Yogyakarta, Javanese dance has taken on new life. Noted choreographers like Bagong Kussudiardja, who once studied with the American dance doyen, Martha Graham, are revitalizing the form. Bold, vibrant new movements, dynamic gamelan compositions and faster pacing, combined with the old elegance and precision, are attracting new audiences and hundreds of dance students.

The new, sophisticated breed of traveler is a prime beneficiary of this resurgence in dance.. The Mardawa Budaya school of Yogyakarta-style dance, one of the most respected in Java, performs for visitors three times weekly at the Dalem Pujokusuman, a small royal family compound near the kraton. Unlike truncated and bastardized "traditional dance performances" in other regions, these new Javanese dances remain artistically valid, no matter where they are performed.

"Yogyakarta-style Javanese dance now has four recognized schools," says Bagong Kussudiardja. "One of these, Sasminto's style, is performed mainly for tourists at Pujokusuman. But it is no less authentic than the others." One modern adaptation is the Sendratari, an acronym of three Indonesian words — seni, drama, tari — meaning art, drama and dance. Essentially Sendratari is a traditional dance drama sans the lengthy dialogues and it has quickly become a Yogyakarta institution.

Fittingly, the most famous venue for Sendratari is the Prambanan itself. There, during the four nights of the full moon, during the dry season months June through September each year, the relief panels of the Ramayana on the sides of the temples are brought to life as hundreds of dancers move elegantly in the jasmine breezes of a Javanese night. Not far away are the paddy fields where the next morning ordinary people will bless the fields with their rhythms.

similar crowd also gathers on Thursday night near the village of Imogiri, 13 kilometers south of Yogyakarta. They climb the 345 stone steps to the hilltop grave of Sultan Agung.

Senopati and Sultan Agung, two of the greatest military heroes of old Java, were the founders of the modern Mataram Empire. Senopati was the son of Kyai Gedhe Pamanahan, a self-styled descendant of the Majapahit kings of East Java, who in turn claimed

zenith of its power and glory by conquering the eastern two thirds of Java. His one defeat, significantly, was at the hands of the Dutch East India Company, the VOC. Though the Dutch initially confined their activities to the coast, during the next 150 years they were increasingly drawn into the Javanese interior.

After Agung's death in 1648, a succession of ineffectual monarchs governed his fragile empire. The perfidies and tyranny of these

descent from the Sanjayas of ancient Mataram. According to the Babad Kraton, a somewhat fanciful historical chronicle, a falling star spoke to Senopati of the rise, glory and subsequent fall of a new Mataram Kingdom while he meditated on the shore of the Southern Ocean. Senopati was then transported to the underwater palace of Loro Kidul, the dreaded female spirit ruler of the Southern Ocean. There he spent three days and nights engaged in meditation and other more sensual pursuits before reemerging to defeat the rival kingdom of Pajang.

Senopati's grandson, Sultan Agung, propelled the Second Mataram Empire to the

rulers severely weakened the new empire.

By the middle of the 18th century, the court had been moved to Surakarta and internal rebellions along with external pressures threatened to destroy the remnants of modern Mataram. The Dutch, who had originally come to Indonesia as merchants, now virtually administered the island's north coast. They even fielded armies to support the reigning monarch, Sunan (Indonesian for "prince") Pakubuono II, in order to maintain Dutch control of Java's external trade.

Into this chaotic scene stepped Prince Mangkubumi, the half-brother of Pakubuono II. Mangkubumi was in many respects the exact opposite of the weak, vacillating and hopelessly incompetent sunan. Much like Indonesia's present government, a Javanese king ruled less by coercion than by seeking and sustaining a consensus from the various societal groups. He

The ubiquitous **warung** *(above) where Yogyakarta's best food is to be found is a common sight in every Indonesian city, town and village. This particular roadside establishment specializes in hot milk and honey with toast for late night snackers.*

relied on the glory of the court rather than brute strength. The power of Javanese king emanated from the mystical properties of the *pusakas*, the royal heirlooms thought to contain powerful ancestral spirits. He also banked on a spirit of cooperation and common interest to secure the loyalty of powerful aristocrats.

Sunan Pakubuono II, under pressure from the VOC, began to make unilateral decisions that affected his entire kingdom. On several

to divide Mataram into two equal kingdoms, each to be ruled by the rival kings. This was accomplished with scrupulous fairness, apportioning the areas household by household. Mangkubumi was given the title Sultan, and took the name Hamengkubuono I, while Pakubuono was called Susuhanan.

In 1755 Mangkubumi and Pakubuono III met in Gijanti, near Mt Lawu, where the former had established a temporary court, to sign the

occasions during Pakubuono II's rule, Mangkubumi upbraided his older brother with the reminder that the role of a ruler carried the obligation to reign only. As the hapless sunan withdrew into the protection of his VOC allies, Mangkubumi donned the traditional mantle of warrior-king and joined his brother princes in rebellion.

In 1749, as control of Mataram was passing from Pakubuono II to his son who became Pakubuono III, Mangkubumi declared himself Pakubuono III and set up a rival court in the village of Jogya, near the early Mataram courts of Plered and Kota Gede.

Thus, Mangkubumi had been recognized as a viable alternative king by his followers, which meant the Dutch could not afford to ignore the rebel monarch. They negotiated with Mangkubumi through a shadowy Turk named Seh Ibrahim and reached an agreement

Treaty of Gijanti. The agreement divided Mataram into the Sultanate of Yogyakarta and the Susuhananate of Surakarta. By signing the treaty, the susuhanan and sultan were put in the unprecedented and acutely uncomfortable position of being two omnipotent monarchs virtually living in the same room.

Appropriately, they sealed the agreement in the European manner by drinking a glass of beer, kissing each other on the cheek, and going to great lengths to ensure that both left the room at exactly the same time. The susuhunan and sultan never met again, and both *kratons* diligently ignored the other's existence for the next two hundred years.

---

*The **Beringhao market** on Jalan Malioboro (**following pages**) is the commercial heart of lower class Yogya. Housewives and servants load up becaks with all manner of food and household goods for the long peddle back to their homes.*

The farmlands of Java *offer a perennial surplus of food. The sidewalk vendors outside the Beringhao market offer a wide variety of fresh tropical fruit from the Yogya lowlands and apples, grapes and other temperate fruit from mountain orchards.*

Nyona Suharti's table groans with Yogyakarta's finest delicacy, Mbak Berek fried chicken. The best food in Yogya is found in unpretentious eateries like Nyona Suharti's and roadside *warungs* all over town.

Boiled Buffalo Hide and Other Delicacies

U nlike other ethnic groups in the region, notably the Chinese, the Javanese do not regard dining as a social occasion. Most prefer to load up a plate with rice, soybean cake, and vegetables and eat alone in a corner.

Nevertheless, dining out in Yogyakarta can be a rewarding activity.

One of the interesting local specialties is gudeg, a sweet mixed mash of jackfruit cooked in coconut milk with eggs and soybean cake.

Gudeg is served over a plate of rice, along with a piece of boiled chicken or a hard boiled egg in a spicy sauce. Adventurous gourmets will be heartened to learn that a piece of boiled buffalo hide sometimes accompanies the dish.

Yogyakarta's other specialty is fried chicken. Mind you, this is not your bland, fat, factory chicken or tasteless fast-food two-piece snack.

Ayam Mbak Berek, named after the woman who invented the dish, uses chicken left free to roam around the yard or kampung. That produces a leaner, slightly tougher but far tastier bird.

The kampung chicken is boiled, then coated with a mixture of coconut and spices according to the cook's private variation on the recipe. It's deep-fried just before serving. Eaten with rice, pungent betai beans, leaves of raw cabbage with sambal (a fiery paste of crushed chili peppers) and washed down with a cold draught of Indonesia's delicious Bintang beer (one of the welcome legacies of Dutch colonialism), Ayam Mbak Berek ranks among the world's best fried chicken meals.

Yogyakarta's best food is generally found on the streets, not in hotels and fancy restaurants. The ubiquitous warung — canvas tents on bamboo frames covering a wooden table and benches — offer a cornucopia of snacks and rice-based meals, made even more delicious by the informal atmosphere. Kaki lima, literally "five feet," are roving hawker carts; the ingenious name refers to the cart's two large wheels, a small support stand, and the owner's two feet. Kaki lima ply the roads and alleyways of Yogyakarta, selling sate, fried rice and noodles, and snacks.

The most popular warung or kaki lima food, sate, reaches mouth-watering perfection in Yogyakarta. Consisting of small pieces of goat or chicken broiled on wooden skewers, sate is usually dipped in a tangy, sweet peanut sauce. The greatest concentration of warung sate is on Jalan Colombo near Gajah Mada University, a popular haunt of students. In addition to sate, a favorite early evening snack served here is boiled mussels and crab. There can be no doubts about their freshness; the live seafood is laid on the warung table — the crabs claws tied shut with twine. Your selection is boiled before your eyes and served with a tangy appetizing chilli sauce.

"When life hands you an unripe mango, make rujak,' is a Javanese aphorism encouraging you to make the best of what you have. Rujak is sliced green mango served with a sweet, very spicy sauce of palm sugar, dried crushed shrimp, and chillies.

Other typical Javanese dishes include ayam opor, chicken simmered in coconut milk; and, gado-gado, a mixture of lightly-cooked vegetables, cubes of boiled glutinous rice, soybean curd, and a hard boiled egg smothered in rich peanut sauce.

Most Javanese have a sweet tooth, so for before, after, or between meals, the Yogyanese have developed an impressive array of sweet snacks, most made with rice flour and palm sugar. Bakpia is a steamed dumpling filled with bean paste, originally a Chinese dish. To wash the snacks down, the Javanese prefer shaved ice sweetened with various syrups in iridescent colors.

Of course, not all the food in Yogyakarta is Javanese. Like all cosmopolitan cities, it offers a range of cuisine from all parts of the archipelago, and elsewhere. One of the most popular is Padang food.

Wherever a Minangkabau man goes, chances are he will likely open a restaurant. And the legions of Minangkabau males who have moved to Yogyakarta from their homeland in Padang, the provincial capital of West Sumatra, have resulted in a plethora of Padang restaurants. These modest eateries are Indonesia's ultimate fast food outlets. Plates of spicy pre-cooked meats and vegetables appear on your table seconds after you sit down.

In any Padang restaurant, the specialties are rendang, buffalo meat cooked in coconut milk; otak, mutton brains in curry; and, several types of curried yard-fed chicken. Load your plate with rice, then take your pick from the various dishes on the table, paying only for what you eat.

Backpackers with a hankering for Western food after grueling months of overland travel through Asia are always pleasantly surprised at the variety of European food available in Yogyakarta. Pasar Kembang, the area of cheap hotels near the railway station, has long boasted several modest establishments serving passable Western fare.

In recent years, a young Yogyanese trained in a Jakarta hotel school has taught several cooks in Pasar Kembang the fine art of French cuisine. You may now enjoy filet poivre and pommes frites et crudites in one of several bamboo and thatch cafes for a ridiculously low price. Unfortunately, because of Indonesia's import tax, a bottle of mediocre wine will cost seven times as much as the entire meal. So you may want to eat your French meal with Dutch beer.

Java's songbirds catch the morning breeze or hang out in the market, waiting to be sold. One bird, perhaps destined for turtledove stardom, regards onlookers with a quizzical air.

Heavenly Songs in the Wind

As the first rays of dawn light the hills around Yogyakarta, a typical Javanese gentleman clad in a colorful batik sarong and cotton T-shirt, pulls on a rope to hoist a bamboo cage on a high pole beside his house. The feathered occupant of the cage, a gray turtledove, enjoys the cool breezes wafting above the roof tops.

If he follows the typical routine of a Javanese gentleman's ideal morning routine, the man may sit on his front stoop for the next three hours, sipping jasmine tea and listening to his dove's gentle songs.

For the Javanese, a turtledove is no mere pet. The Java Turtledove, Geopelia striata, Perkutut in Indonesian, is highly-regarded, a heavenly symbol. To be fulfilled, a Javanese gentleman requires only a house, a wife, a kris, and a turtledove.

The island's fascination with turtledoves dates back centuries. The anatomical terms used to describe a turtledove's magic powers originated in the Hindu religion, indicating that doves already had mystical connotations during the great Hindu empires of Java. Historical records indicate King

Brawijaya of the 13th century Majapahit Empire was a turtledove enthusiast.

Depending on the bird's coloration and physical characteristics, a turtledove may possess the power to repel black magic, ensure good crops and even to make the owner attractive to the opposite sex. But ornamentation aside, the turtledove's real attraction is the sounds it makes.

Bird-fanciers the world over acclaim the Java Turtledove for its song, which is actually the mating call of the male. The bird sings continuously from dawn to midday and intermittently from mid-afternoon until nightfall. Some birds sing during the night, but these are shunned as bringers of misfortune.

The most dulcet-toned birds hail from East Java. It's said that life is harder in that arid region, which gives its birds a more plaintive call.

After buying a young dove, the owner employs a variety of means to train the bird to add depth and tonality to its song. A young dove is often placed in a succession of cages, to determine which colors and configurations make him most comfortable and produce the best tone.

Nor is a dove's training entirely traditional. Today many an owner will tape his pet's call over days or weeks. Then he splices the best sequences together like a record producer to make one perfect song, which he will then play near the cage, in the hope that the dove will imitate the revised melody.

While working on his hit song, a dove is pampered, fed with herbs and Java's famous herbal medicine, jamu, to clear its throat and stimulate its appetite. The bird is also entertained with soft whistles and gentle words from the doting owner.

When the dove is deemed ready for competition, it is massaged, bathed and driven — ideally in an air-conditioned Mercedes — to a contest, where birds are judged on precision, perfect pitch and general comportment. Major contenders have a shot at the Hamengkubuwono IX cup competition held biannually during the second week of August.

The scientific breeding of turtledoves began during the 1960s. At that time, Thai enthusiasts imported Javanese birds, which they believe have the best song, to cross breed with Thai doves, which are considered to possess better tonal quality. The new breeds were soon exported back to Java, where enthusiasts continue to refine the breed.

For a Javanese just owning a turtledove is its own reward. But a well trained bird can be lucrative as well.

Sultan Hamengkubuwono VII (1877-1921) would grant large tracts of land in exchange for a fine turtledove. In modern times, a standard trained dove sells for about US$200, while a top competition winner can change hands for as much as US$10,000.

After signing the Treaty of Gijanti, Mangkubumi embarked on a massive construction program in his capital, which was now known by the more resounding name of Yogyakarta. Most of the city's major landmarks and tourist attractions date from this time when Mangkubumi, like his predecessors, sought to anchor the legitimacy of his kingdom in mortar and stone. He built his *kraton* and, nearby, the pleasure palace of Taman Sari, and put massive walls around the entire complex. A two-kilometer ceremonial boulevard, now called Jalan Malioboro, led from the Kraton's main gate north to a 22-meter tall Tugu monument, a phallic stone on which the Sultan could gaze in meditation from his throne room.

The Dutch had a construction program of their own. As part of their agreement with Mangkubumi, the latter was to build them a fortress flanking the boulevard north of the Alun-Alun, the large ceremonial field in front of the Kraton. Mangkubumi complied with the request, although the construction schedule was a prime example of Javanese procrastination, taking some decades to complete. Later, when the Dutch built the resident's mansion across the boulevard from the fortress, the reigning Sultan had to endure the humbling experience of meditating on his Tugu while staring between the two most blatant symbols of foreign domination of his kingdom. Whether by pure chance or design, the Dutch had learned to utilize the Javanese penchant for mystic symbolism.

When he wanted to retire completely from the pressures of running a kingdom and dealing with the Dutch, Mangkubumi could enter Taman Sari, his pleasure palace. Today Taman Sari is a tumbledown collection of crumbling mortar, overrun by squatters and batik painters and it takes a vivid imagination to picture the former grandeur and ingenuity of the complex. In Mangkubumi's day, it was a maze of underwater tunnels and structures that rose majestically from an artificial lake. Other than its function as a royal playground, Taman Sari was reputedly linked by a tunnel to the southern ocean, 26 kilometers away, making it a symbol that legitimized Mangkubumi's claim on the throne. Like his an-

Yogyanese can indulge their collective sweet tooth with a cornucopia of cakes and candies, most prepared from the same basic ingredients: glutinous rice and palm sugar. Other sweetmeats include those made from peanut, coconut and banana.

cestor Senopati, Mangkubumi exploited the mystic connection with the Queen of the Southern Seas.

The Central Javanese and their distant cousins, the Balinese, are basically agrarian people who distrust the sea — with good reason. The crashing breakers from the Indian ocean and vicious crosscurrents and undertows off beaches like Parangtritis make the Southern Seas the abode of spirits and demons, a place to be avoided. An area of gray sand dunes Parangtritis is the domain of Nyai Loro Kidul, Queen of the South Seas.

Senopati declared that he could call upon the spirit armies of the dreaded Queen of the South Seas to defeat his enemies. According to legend, Nyai Loro Kidul was a princess of the Pajajaran kingdom in West Java who was cursed by her father for refusing a dynastic marriage and banished to rule over the South-

ern Sea. Loro Kidul and her female spirit army occasionally bathe in the fresh water springs at Parangtritis where they are said to seduce passing males.

All subsequent sultans have sustained the royal connections with the spirits of the Southern Seas. Even today, the reigning sultan symbolically marries Loro Kidul every year after the mystic Bedoyo, one of the Kraton's most sacred dances. And in one of Yogyakarta's most compelling ceremonies, Labuhan, palace officials carry clippings of the magically-powerful hair and nails of the sultan to the sea as a symbolic offering to Loro Kidul.

The industrious pot salesman (above) might push his leaden bicycle along many kilometers of back country roads each day. On the other hand, the pampered Komodo dragon resident at Gembira Loka Zoo (right) will only twitch a muscle at feeding time.

In Mataram, the successors of a powerful monarch rarely had their predecessor's strengths. Mangkubumi's descendants were no exception. Mangkubumi's son, Hamengkubuono II, possessed little of his father's ability to balance opposing forces and interests for the benefit of his kingdom. His failure to deal with internal squabbles and external pressure weakened Yogyakarta.

As dissension fragmented the court, the last great historical figure, Prince Diponegoro, a son of Sultan Hamengkubuono II. Diponegoro disdained the corruption and artificiality of the Yogyakarta court and moved to the countryside. There he forged solid links with the religious community and peasantry while retaining his hereditary connection with the highest aristocracy.

By this time Central Java had entered a period of instability. The Dutch had become

Dutch seized every opportunity to augment their own influence. When the arrogant Hamengkubuono II attempted to defy the Europeans, they responded with military force. The *kraton* was invaded twice, once by the Dutch under Willem Daendels, then by the English under Stamford Raffles. These outrages of their virtually-sacred royal institution deeply humiliated the Yogyanese. Lacking an effective leader to counter Europe's industrial might, ancient, mystic Java was fast fading into the mists of the past.

But in the 1820s, legend has it that the Queen of the Southern Seas surfaced one more time to lend a helping hand to Mataram's

deeply involved in the economy of Yogyakarta, working with wealthy Chinese residents to lease large tracts of land from impoverished nobles for coffee and sugar plantations. If the Yogyanese aristocracy were contemptuous of the pasty-faced Europeans, the foreigners were no less contemptuous of the common Javanese and their customs. Demands by tax collectors and tollgate keepers that verged on extortion caused hardship and social disruption. In 1822, Hamengkubuono III died; it was rumored that he had been poisoned. At the end of that year Mt. Merapi erupted; as always, that was regarded as a portent of disaster. Sure enough the hammer fell in 1823, at least for the nobles. The governor-general abolished the titles to all private leaseholds. Although this benefited the common Javanese, many nobles who had leased the land now were suddenly deprived of their sole

Garish movie posters (above) are often more entertaining than the films they advertise. These huge canvases are a popular art form in themselves, and is a means of livelihood for the many otherwise unemployed art school graduates.

income and went heavily into debt.

As far as Prince Diponegoro was concerned, it was time for action. During a pilgrimage to Senopati's tomb at Kota Gede, Sultan Agung's resting place at Imogiri, and other holy places of the Mataram Empire, Diponegoro had a series of visions which convinced him that he was destined to be the future king of Java. Like his illustrious ancestors, Diponegoro was said to have been visited by Loro Kidul. She

exiled to Sulawesi. In honor of Diponegoro's heroics, the Indonesian government has reconstructed his house in Tegelrejo, fashioning a monument and museum there that commemorates the Java War. Paintings depict the original structure in flames during the unsuccessul attempt to arrest Diponegoro. Attendants proudly indicate a hole in a brick wall that Diponegoro supposedly smashed with his bare fist so he and his followers could escape.

promised him divine aid to unite the island and eject the foreigners.

On May 20, 1825, after a period of tension between Diponegoro and his enemies in the court, Dutch troops attempted to arrest Diponegoro at his house in Tegelrejo, 6.4 kilometers from Yogyakarta. Diponegoro and his retainers fought off the Dutch and fled, beginning five years of rebellion.

Initially, Diponegoro's guerrilla war had the full support of the populace and chalked up a series of successes. They inflicted heavy losses on the Dutch. Most other regional Javanese princes opposed the rebels, however, and sent troops to assist the Europeans.

This aid from the allied princes and more effective deployment of Dutch troops turned the war against the rebels by 1827. In 1830 a harried Diponegoro was lured into negotiation with the Dutch, then promptly captured and

Although the Indonesians regard the Java War as the first major independence movement, a precursor of this century's revolutionary struggle, Diponegoro's long insurrection was actually a conservative backlash. Instead of engineering a leap forward into freedom, the prince tried to reverse the colonial tide and revive the feudal antecedents of Mataram's years of glory. He did not realize that the Dutch, through their heavy-handed interference in the economy, had irrevocably altered the old Java. Diponegoro was doomed to fail; 70 years would pass before the Javanese would learn to use the social changes wrought by the Dutch to their own advantage.

An imported popular medium, film draws some inspiration from Java's indigenous entertainment form, wayang. *Conversely, some* wayang *puppet masters draw on the techniques of film, playing down philosophy and morals for blood and guts action.*

48

The high walls of the *kraton* that still stand in Yogyakarta reflect the military power of the 18th century Mataram kingdom, but the modern *kraton's* interior reflects the rapid erosion of that power after the Java War. After it came under total Dutch domination, the Yogyakarta court turned inward, focusing its attention on the cultivation of the arts and old customs. In typical Javanese fashion, the Sultans came to terms with their political impotence by adopting the culture of their alien overlords. The *kraton* is an intriguing melange of European and local architectural styles: Italian marble, crystal chandeliers, and cast iron columns in a classically Javanese setting. Bandstands, complete with stained glass paintings of western musical instruments stand in front of a pavilion carved with symbols from Javanese Hinduism and Islam.

Today, most court ceremonies and daily life within the *kraton* remain virtually unchanged from the days of Mangkubumi. During the week of celebrations leading up to the birthday of the Islamic prophet Mohammad, the sultan leads great royal processions around the Alun-Alun. Mountains of rice sculpted to resemble mythical Mt. Meru are paraded about, then distributed to the people.

These ceremonies are not a re-enactment of bygone glory merely for the sake of tourists. The costumed attendants of the sultan, armed with spears, take their duties seriously. When they are not participating in such royal spectacles, the court·retainers, barefoot and clad in full Javanese costume of batik sarong, *blangkon* (headdress), *surjan* (jacket) and a kris held by a cummerbund in the back, escort tourists though the outer pavilions of the palace. Or they pass time in photogenic repose in courtyard terraces.

The anachronisms of the modern *kraton* do not represent a rejection of the 20th century as much as a casual indifference to the modern age. The Javanese have a talent, some say genius, of incorporating only those aspects of foreign influence which will enhance their own culture and way of life. In many areas of Yogyanese life, modern technology and social concepts have been wholeheartedly adopted. But in the microcosmic world of the *kraton*, few aspects of the 20th century have any validity, so they are ignored.

During the latter part of the 19th century, the members of the court occupied themselves with refining their classic arts, especially dance and the wayang, to an effete and artificial perfection, while Yogyakarta's elite in general applied their energy to refining their own lives. The Dutch used idle aristocrats as functionaries in their bureaucracy. With their military traditions completely frustrated and their aristocracy co-opted into the Dutch colonial apparatus, the Yogyanese made a virtue of introversion; they developed an intricate, sophisticated set of values, attitudes and etiquette that to this day have remained the centerpiece of Yogyanese life.

The most obvious aspect of this Javanese cultural sophistication involves social behavior. Even a casual visitor to Yogyakarta will notice the high level of courtesy and refinement the Yogyanese display in daily life. Of course, this is partly born of necessity. Impolite and aggressive behavior might otherwise spawn violence in Yogyakarta's cramped living conditions. Thus, social grace is the surface manifestation of the Javanese effort to develop inner peace and harmony. If, through refined social behavior, a Javanese can prevent the stimulation of base emotions, he will be more successful in cultivating and developing his inner spirit, the *batin*. This spiritual cultivation, *kebatinan*, is by its nature a private affair, but it occasionally manifests itself in colorful events that visitors are welcome to attend. One favorite venue for *kebatinan* practices is Parangtritis, the beach 28 kilometers south of Yogyakarta. In a typical ceremony, a man dressed in full traditional Javanese costume and shaded by a parasol sits on the iron-gray sand surrounded by attendants. Although he could be a member of the court or aristocracy, he might just as often be a small businessman or professional soliciting financial advice from the Queen of the Southern Seas. To communicate with Loro Kidul, a mystic sits cross-legged by the water's edge with an assistant behind him and prays.

After several minutes of prayer, a wave suddenly washes over the mystic. He leans into it, his face submerged in the churning water. The assistant embraces the mystic from behind, then half-carries, half-drags him to the supplicant, who holds out a piece of yellow cloth. The old mystic spits out a mouthful of seawater onto the cloth, which the supplicant reverently places into a carved wooden box. Later, assistants cast scatter jasmine flowers on the surface of the sea. Into the waves, they cast offerings of fruit which are immediately snatched up by waiting villagers.

Characters from the **wayang kulit** *puppet theater are found throughout Javanese popular culture. In this poster, which advertises a football championship match, two* wayang *clowns, Petruk and Bagong, are portrayed arguing over the rules of football.*

The Sacred Dagger

No Javanese gentleman would consider himself well-dressed unless he had a kris tucked into the cummerbund of his traditional Javanese costume.

But this famed, wavy-bladed dagger is not just a fashion accessory. It's a status symbol and object of veneration. The kris is nothing less than a necessity in the life of a Javanese man.

The kris dates back to the island's earliest recorded history — West Java's shadowy Pajajaran kingdom which had its roots in a 5th century Hindu state. By the time ancient Mataram was rising in the 7th century, kris-making was an established art, though the blade at that point was basic and unadorned.

The development of the kris flowered during Mataram's modern era. Although it was an Islamic state, its people were heavily-influenced by its earlier Hindu-Buddhist manifestation and believed that the spirits of their ancestors inhabited certain items in the kraton. These royal heirlooms, known as the pusaka, were regarded as the foundation of royal power.

Given the militaristic nature of the Mataram Javanese, the kris ranked among the most important type of pusaka. As a result it attained equal importance in the social and mystic life outside the palace.

After the division of Mataram into Yogyakarta and Surakarta in the middle of the 18th century, kris-making was no longer the reserve of court craftsmen. The growing numbers of kris makers, known as empu, began to concentrate on aesthetic values rather than supernatural considerations.

Kris-making was an arcane and exacting art. Blades were forged by heating and folding alternate layers of meteorite iron and nickel. Then the kris was treated with a mixture of arsenic, lemon juice and coconut water to blacken the iron and whiten the nickel, bringing out the damascene patterns.

Today, these patterns are looked at upon as indicators of the spiritual characteristics of a kris. For instance, the owner of a kris with a wavy line down the center of the blade will have no difficulty making a living, while a blade with a coconut leaf pattern can save its owner's life.

However, a kris only performs these functions if it is spiritually in tune with its owner. Consequently, a person who owns an incompatible kris can suffer grave misfortune. And a kris that is purchased, rather than handed down from generation to generation or presented as a gift, automatically loses all supernatural power.

In modern Yogyakarta, the kris is used in most life cycle rites in the belief it can ward off disaster. It also plays a significant role in many ceremonies, including those revolving around the harvests and at factory openings, to help insure success.

Kebatinan practices did not make the Yogyanese into a society of hermits and ascetics. Just as some Javanese still dabble in mystic disciplines to gain wealth or other favors, many Yogyanese today used the rites associated with *kebatinan* early in the 20th century to prepare themselves for a much more important task — securing their freedom from the Dutch.

Although the Dutch and Javanese bureaucrats enjoyed peace and prosperity during the 100 years of direct Dutch control over the East Indies, an awakening national consciousness boiled under the gracious veneer of Dutch colonialism, seething as ominously as the elemental forces inside the outwardly tranquil Merapi volcano that dominates Yogyakarta's pastoral backdrop. The nationalists shrewdly took advantage of the educational opportunities offered by the Dutch as part of their liberal "Ethical Policy." They used the academic training to prepare themselves for the day when the Dutch would be gone.

In 1942 the Japanese swept through Southeast Asia and into the East Indies, defeating the Dutch colonial defenders with embarrassing ease. Although the Japanese Occupation was a great hardship, it also provided a golden opportunity for Indonesian nationalism. When the Japanese interned the Dutch nationals, the educated native nationalists were placed in positions of bureaucratic responsibility that they had previously been denied. During the next three years, the Javanese elite gained self-confidence while the nationalist leaders prepared the groundwork for the independence that they were sure would follow the Japanese pull-out.

On August 17, 1945, two days after the Japanese surrender, Indonesia declared itself an independent nation. The Dutch returned and tried to reclaim their lost colony in the face of fanatical resistance. During the subsequent four years of chaos, Yogyakarta had one more sojourn in the historical limelight. The Indonesian Republican government moved its capital from Batavia to Yogyakarta in January, 1946, because the Republicans were coming under increasing military pressure from the Dutch.

During the next 18 months, Republicans from all areas of the archipelago flocked to

Squat and solid, Borobudur sits in the rice fields near Yogya. Borobudur itself is actually a small hill encased in two million cubic feet of stone. The new system of drainage ducts and waterproofing prevents the supporting earth from being eroded by rainwater.

Yogyakarta, swelling the population and severely straining facilities. When the Dutch blockaded Indonesia and besieged Yogyakarta in May, 1947, the Yogyanese had to rely solely on their own meager resources in their fight for freedom.

During the next year, Yogyakarta truly earned its sobriquet of "Revolutionary City." Like Paris in 1872 or Barcelona in 1936, the revolutionary atmosphere obliterated social

Gunawan, Sujana Kerton and other pioneering painters formed the Pelukis Front, an association of artists dedicated to documenting the Revolutionary struggle.

Neither could Affandi, the notoriously non-political, neo-expressionist now recognized as Indonesia's leading artist, remain aloof from the revolutionary fervor. Cajoled into joining the Pelukis Front as they painted the Dutch positions near Yogyakarta and suddenly

differences as the people struggled for a common goal. Yogyakarta residents greeted each other in passing with phrases such as: "Revolt! Brother," or, for the more long-winded "Don't forget August 17th, 1945, the day of our Independence!" As starvation loomed, anyone could approach any house and be assured of receiving a share, however small, of the available food. Most people were dressed in rags, or if they were lucky, in old rice sacks, because imports of cloth had been halted since the Japanese Occupation.

Even during these dark times, art and culture were not forgotten. In the hot, dusty streets of besieged Yogyakarta, Hendra

The baroque ornamentation of the *kraton extends even to the nearby Great Mosque. The clock gives the time for Islamic prayer, sometimes up to one half hour off Standard Time. It is here at the Great Mosque that the Garebeg Procession finally ends up.*

caught up in the revolutionary spirit, he leaped from cover, shouting: "If I die, I die." Then he madly sketched the Dutch soldiers in the distance as they looked on bemused.

When they were not bravely risking the ridicule of Dutch troops, the Pelukis Front artists used their brushes to portray the hard life in Yogyakarta itself. Sketch pads in hand, they documented the poverty, the forced squalor brought on by the scarcity of essential goods, and the dignity and pride of a people suffering for an ideal.

Unfortunately, few of the remarkable wartime paintings have survived. During the Second Police Action, when the Dutch occupied Yogyakarta, Hendra and the other artists decided to flee, as they knew they would be imprisoned or executed for their propaganda activities. Hendra gave most of the Pelukis Front paintings to a neighbor who buried them in her backyard. Later, the monsoon rains soaked into the ground and destroyed all of the paintings.

Yet another notable revolutionary firebrand in Yogyakarta lent inspiration to the resistance — the sultan himself, Hamengkubuono IX. In 1939, the elderly Sultan Hamengkubuono VIII had recalled his son from school in the Netherlands. Shortly after returning, his father passed away and the young man became

International pressure finally forced the Dutch to end their attempt to recolonize Indonesia and relinquish their claim on the East Indies once and for all. In 1950, the Republican government moved back to Jakarta, as Batavia was renamed, and Yogyakarta again sank back into its slow, genteel way of life. Because it has few natural resources, Yogyakarta became an economic backwater, sharing only tangentially in Indonesia's

Sultan Hamengkubuono IX. The new sultan bided his time during the Japanese Occupation, then after independence instituted wide-ranging reforms in his Sultanate.

Drafting his counterpart, the Paku Alam, as his administrative assistant, Hamengkubuono IX stripped the crusty old court bureaucracy of many prerogatives and privileges. Paku Alam moved the officials from the countryside into the *kraton* where they could safeguard old traditions to their heart's content while the sultan revamped local administration to cope with the chaotic conditions of post-colonial Yogyakarta. Because he enjoyed immense personal prestige, the sultan managed to form a private army, briefly reviving the ancient Javanese tradition of rallying behind a military king. After 200 years, the Yogyakarta *Kraton* finally housed a worthy successor to Mangkubumi.

prosperity during the past quarter century.

But if circumstance has diminished Yogyakarta's economic role, the same conditions also helped turn the city into the vanguard of Indonesian culture. The low cost of living (the amount of money you spend in a day in Jakarta lasts at least a week in Yogyakarta) coupled with the city's traditionally revolutionary character has created a mecca for Indonesia's artists and intelligentsia, and turned Yogyakarta into Indonesia's social and cultural laboratory. "What do you want to do?' local choreographer and painter Bagong Kussudiardja often asks visitors, somewhat rhetorically. "Start up a new social system, try

*This **kraton** facade looks toward the Alun-Alun, the main town square. The ornamentation on the facade of the* kraton *is relatively new as it was finished during a general restoration of the* kraton *proper during the 1930s.*

Yogya's Handy Craftsmen

Since the 18th century, the artistically-oriented Kraton has encouraged the development of handicrafts in Yogyakarta. The ceremonial needs of the palace itself had a direct bearing on the rise of expertise in the creation of batik and silverwork, while leathercraft developed as an offshoot of wayang shadow puppetry.

Today, handicrafts give the people of Yogya a chance to express their artistic talent and inventiveness. Unfortunately, it also grants equal opportunity for some to make shameless copies of excellent originals and pass off inferior work to naive foreigners. So when shopping for handicrafts in Yogyakarta, you should visit the upmarket, fixed-price shops first for a look at quality work and its prices, before wandering into the beckoning alleyways of Taman Sari.

Batik is Yogyakarta's best-known handicraft. The process of tracing designs on cloth in wax, then dyeing the unwaxed portions was invented during the 18th century when the import of high-quality cloth from India and Europe began providing workable material.

Originally, batik was an exclusive preserve of the kraton and nobility. But at the beginning of the 20th century it moved out to small private factories south of the kraton.

The word batik is derived from the Javanese term, ntik. It means to make dots and is an apt description of batik-making. In the original process, called batik tulis, designs are laboriously drawn by hand and molten wax is applied to the outline with a canting, a type of pen. The cloth is then dipped in dye, which colors only the unwaxed portions. Afterwards, the wax is boiled out, and the long process repeated for each color of dye.

Because of the prodigious labor involved, only the aristocracy could afford batik. Thus, the textiles evolved into an indicator of social status, in which certain designs were reserved for the various segments of the court.

However, in the late 19th century, a technical innovation, the batik stamp or cap, enabled batik to be mass-produced. The stamp, made of fine copper wire, is dipped in wax, then continually applied to the cloth, producing a repetitive pattern, but greatly lowering the price.

Most of today's batik is produced using this batik cap process. Although some traditional artists still produce hand-drawn batik, primarily for formal men's shirts, many traditional batik tulis artists have given way to fashion designers who produce trendy, high-priced garments sold exclusively in boutiques.

For various reasons, specific villages in Java

become almost exclusively associated with a specific handicraft. On the north coast, Jepara is known for its wood carving and Cirebon for its rattan work.

Nearer Yogyakarta, Kota Gede is Java's silver headquarters. Although Bali's silver designs are often more inventive, the Kota Gede craftsmen produce silverwork of 838 and 925 purity that generally is of a higher overall quality. Popular serious purchases include tea sets, dinner ware and jewelry. For souvenirs, there are miniature becaks and andongs. Kota Gede's silversmiths even have something for expatriate oilmen — silver hard hats etched with oil derricks and pipelines.

Arguably, Yogyakarta's oldest craft, the making of wayang kulit puppets, is not strictly leatherwork; the buffalo skin is dried into stiff parchment instead of being tanned into soft leather. A standard-size figure takes at least ten days to make at a cost of U.S.$20 to $50 for gold-leaf finishing.

Most wayang carvers, strictly adhere to established designs which in Yogyakarta are defined by the palace. A few other artists are now experimenting with innovative and controversial wayang designs. During the past two decades, Yogya's wayang carvers have expanded their output to the production of consumer goods such as wallets and suitcases.

Unfortunately, working with the stiff parchment of wayang puppets has ill-prepared them to fashion soft and supple high-quality leather. Most goods hawked on Jalan Malioboro are pretty shoddy and have substandard finishing. But the quality is slowly improving.

One interesting offshoot of leathercraft and an example of Yogyakarta's cosmopolitan flavor are leather-trimmed rattan bags, purses and suitcases that now appear in exclusive shops.

Used rattan with bold graphic designs is bought from Dayaks in East Kalimantan, then cut and trimmed with Yogyanese leather to produce these creations that could well be called Yogya Gucci.

Five kilometers outside of Yogyakarta on the road to Bantul, the village of Kasongan has a tradition of making terracotta pots. A few years ago, some of Yogyakarta's major artists and sculptors descended on the village and encouraged the local craftsmen to adopt new designs.

The figures now show the Yogyanese love of whimsy and fantasy. Horses, tigers, elephants and birds, all by untrained artists, make interesting and inexpensive souvenirs. Unfortunately, the lightly-fired clay is very fragile and hard to get home in one piece. Although the pottery can be double-fired on request, it loses its characteristic earth tone and becomes dull black.

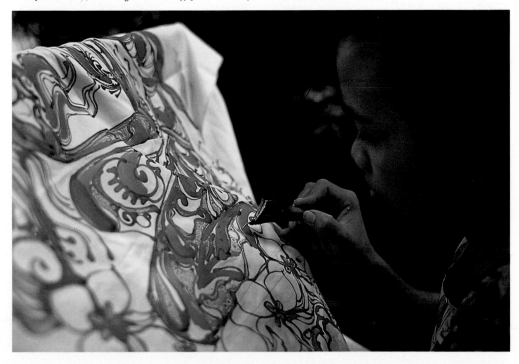

out a new art form or dance style? Yogyakarta is open to almost anything."

Cultural vigor and experimentation is most evident in the arts. Unlike other cultures where traditional and modern forms of expression seem to be at loggerheads, in Yogyakarta the old and new walk the same road and frequently cross paths of influence. Traditional dance draws from modern techniques, while contemporary art looks to traditional culture for inspiration.

Oil painting is currently one of the most dynamic arts. While literature, dance and the wayang flourished under the sultans, painting and sculpture decayed. Islam prohibits the representation of human figures, so art in Yogyakarta was sidetracked into ornamentation like that found on carved chests and mirrors, and calligraphy. Only in the 1920s did Indonesia's artists begin experimenting with

western painting styles. Unfortunately, most tended to emulate the predominant style of the time, *Moie Indie* ("Beautiful Indies"), which depicted lush ricefields, dusky maidens, and, serenely, puffing volcanoes, exclusively for the consumption of tourists and Dutch colonialists returning to Europe.

However, during the Japanese Occupation, the revolution and the early, chaotic years of the republic, Yogyakarta became the headquarters of new movements in Indonesian art, as artists experimented with combinations of old and new. Affandi, when asked to paint recruitment posters for labor gangs, depicted skeletal workers slaving in a tropical hellhole.

Iwan Sagito's paintings, which often depict wayang puppets metamorphosing into humans, explore the boundaries between myth and reality. Many of Yogya's other talented young artists also draw their source of inspiration from traditional culture.

After the revolution, Hendra Gunawan and Sudarso formed Pelukis Rakyat, an artistic cooperative in Yogyakarta that had the objective of experimenting with new art and trying to raise artistic consciousness in the people themselves. Like the Pelukis Front canvasses, most of the early paintings produced by Pelukis Rakyat did not survive. One afternoon, while the entire membership of the cooperative was painting landscapes out of town, some local community residents entered the unlocked house. Tired of being dressed in rags and old rice sacks since 1942, they stripped the canvasses from the walls and made them into trousers and frocks. The residents had taken Pelukis Rakyat's philosophy of "art for the people" literally.

Though the people of Yogya now prefer to collect art for their houses instead of their wardrobe, the city retains its tradition of artistic innovation. The city's artists are currently among those at the vanguard in the search for an Indonesian artistic identity.

One Yogyanese artist who blends European technique and Javanese tradition to startling effect is Iwan Sagito. Originally from Malang, East Java, Iwan moved to Yogyakarta in 1975. He entered the Yogyakarta Fine Arts Institute (ASRI), in 1979 and graduated in 1985. For the past several years, Iwan has been producing compelling, and often disturbing canvasses of high quality. One of Iwan's favorite motifs is the *wayang* puppet, particularly the three dimensional, wooden Golek figures. "When I look at *wayang* puppets, I think that we are like *wayang* puppets. As the puppets are controlled by a *dalang*, we are equally controlled by God," he says.

Another Yogyanese art form continues to generate controversy. Some observers regard the batik painters colony in Taman Sari as the home of scores of aspiring young artists experimenting with an indigenous Yogyanese art form, while others decry the area as a hangout for untalented louts churning out tawdry souvenir paintings.

There is some truth to both viewpoints. Batik painting, a hybrid art form developed by Bagong Kussudiardja during the late 1940s as a way of keeping Yogyakarta's revolutionary youth occupied, has been adopted as the traditional art form of Yogyakarta and a response to traditional Balinese art. Although

Along the backroads of the Yogyakarta Special Region, life often seems as in centuries past, like this scene of a family journeying home from the market. Except that a closer inspection of their goods might reveal modern or Western amenities.

most modern batik painting with its repetitive themes and sloppy execution is, unquestionably, of little artistic merit, a few of Taman Sari's young artists do produce some interesting, albeit predominantly decorative, work. In Yogyakarta, however, decorative art is recognized as a wholly honorable and worthwhile field.

One art form that is attracting increasing interest is an adaptation of traditional theater. The *ketoprak*, which originated in Yogyakarta in the 1920s, is a sort of common man's version of the wayang. It has plots based on folk stories rooted in recorded history rather than Hindu-era mythology as in the *wayang*. Less stylized than *wayang*, the dialogue is generally improvised around a storyline, and the acting similar to 19th century American melodramas.

Ketoprak is still greatly appreciated by the villagers and touring troupes play several times a year in Alun-Alun. Now, the ever-active Yogyakarta artistic community is experimenting with this form, using traditional techniques to relate modern stories. The new performances of Jack Sampoerno's Theater Gandrik, for example, would more likely relate the story of a Yogyakarta youth trying to find employment than the tale of a grasscutter from the court of ancient Majapahit marrying a princess and becoming king.

Yogyakarta is also a hothouse of social experimentation. A notable city landmark is Kampung Code, formerly a deteriorating collection of shacks clinging precariously to the banks of the Code River. A few years ago, the people of this neighborhood, which is run as a cooperative, rebuilt their homes with the assistance of Romo Mangunjaya, a Catholic priest who taught architecture at Gajah Mada University until ten years ago.

Romo Mangunjaya, who left academic life to become a social activist, encouraged the inhabitants of Kampung Code to renovate the community themselves, without waiting for government assistance. Romo Mangunjaya drew up imaginative designs for new houses using local construction materials and techniques. Now Kampung Code is a multi-leveled, bank of airy houses and open communal spaces, a marvel of practical planning. This being Yogyakarta, there is also an artistic touch. The residents enlisted art students to help them paint their new dwellings in bold, graphic designs.

Sadly, local civil servants were not impressed. Claiming the people of Kampung Code lacked discipline, they insisted that all houses should be a uniform color. Apparently what is

60

acceptable in an art gallery in not acceptable on the roadside near a major shopping district. Even in Yogyakarta, municipal authorities remain as shortsighted and unimaginative as they do almost everywhere else in the world.

Despite occasional bureaucratic obfuscation, the character of Yogyakarta is changing. The Yogyanese themselves are increasingly aware that they must take more control of their own lives to fully take advantage of Indonesia's new prosperity.

Partly influenced by the significant non-Javanese population of Yogyakarta, the Yogyanese are becoming more sophisticated in business and economics. The more than 10,0000 entrepreneurial Minangkabau who have migrated from the home villages in West Sumatra to Yogyakarta and many other cities in search of their fortunes have encouraged the Yogyanese to apply sound new business techniques to their operation. Whereas, for example, ten years ago a gallery owner would spend his commission as soon as he received it, now he will probably put some money in the bank with an eye to expanding his gallery.

The government is helping out as well. Small tourist-oriented businesses, primarily restaurants, can now apply for low-interest loans. Much of the current improvement around the tourist areas of Pasar Kembang and Jalan Malioboro was facilitated by government assistance.

Happily for potential visitors, Yogyakarta's future seems likely to be little different from the present. The airport in neighboring Solo, rather than Yogya, is slated to be upgraded to international status. So most new industry is likely to develop around Yogyakarta's erstwhile rival city.

Certainly, tourism will continue grow, with the attendant rampant commercialism. But Yogyakarta's charm is based on an age-old character that is in little danger of radical alteration from foreign influence. Even the occasional young Yogyanese who forsakes his own culture and adopts western dress or manners is regarded, with great condescension, as a "korban mode," a victim of fashion.

Indeed, Yogyakarta has always done things its own way. It takes only what it needs from the world outside, and is charting its own easy-going course into the next century.

The traditional headgear of the palace courtiers illustrates the varied cultural influences that make up Yogyanese court culture and demonstrates the Javanese talent of assimilating outside influences to the benefit of their own culture.

Traditionally, "shadow play", or *wayang* is viewed from behind the screen, where the spectator sees only shadows cast by the puppets. Modern audiences, however, prefer to sit behind the dalang to see the rich decorations on the figures.

Out of the Shadows

One of Java's most sophisticated arts, the shadow puppet theater known as wayang kulit, remains as vital and popular a part of the island's culture as it was centuries ago.

Wayang kulit *involves the manipulation of flat leather puppets. Its subsidiary forms are* wayang golek, *which uses three-dimensional wooden puppets,* wayang wong, *in which human actors perform, and* wayang topeng, *a form in which the actors wear masks.*

Whatever form they take, wayang *performances are equal parts entertainment, morality play and contemporary satire. The basic story lines pit good versus evil, and the former invariably triumphs.*

However, the characters in wayang *do not represent people as much as they embody human characteristics. The good guys are referred to as* halus. *They possess prized Javanese values like humility and self control.*

Halus *puppets have refined features and wiry builds, much like the island's aristocrats.*

The villainous characters are kasar — *loud, uncouth, and repulsive. Most* kasar *of all are the demons: they have round staring eyes and gaping mouths. During a* wayang *performance, the good puppets stand on a bamboo log to the right of the* dalang, *the puppet master; the bad are on his left.*

Wayang *stories are derived from the ancient epics of India, the* Mahabharata *and* Ramayana. *Most portray episodes in a long feud between two families, the Pandawas and Kurawas.*

The complex plots usually revolve around the marriage of some wayang *character, contests to win a gift from the gods, or power struggles that result from the death of a statesman. Backed by a light, the* dalang *masterfully manipulates the flat puppets behind a small screen. The light casts fast-moving shadows of the puppets on the screen, creating the illusion of a spectacle of royal audience scenes, full-scale battles and elaborate ceremonies.*

The first historical mention of wayang *appears in 907 A.D. in writings of the Mataram empire. "Sagaligi presented a wayang performance for the gods, telling the story of the birth of Bima."*

This simple announcement was followed the next century by the first recorded critique of the art form: "How stupid the audience is, to become so involved with the actions of leather puppets on a screen as though they were real people." Apparently, this rather unimaginative critic was one of the few people in history who was not captivated by a wayang performance.

Fortunately, in those days as in modern times, people ignored the critics. The popularity of wayang *steadily increased during subsequent centuries. And with the added innovation of moveable arms on the puppets in the 16th century,* wayang kulit *began evolving into its contemporary form.*

During the same era Islam arrived and supplanted the Hindu precepts of Java's empires, forcing other changes in the wayang. *Because Islam forbids the use of the human figure in art, the realistic shapes of the puppets became highly-stylized. During the long process of refinement, each nuance in the puppet's dress, expression and posture attained deep significance.*

Consequently, like other idiosyncrasies of Javanese culture, the wayang *is difficult for Westerners to grasp immediately. Though the word* wayang *now refers to the entire art form, it originally meant shadow and encompassed only the shadow puppet shows. The audience traditionally sat behind the screen, watching the flickering shadows cast by the puppets.*

Perhaps that's appropriate. A foreign spectator who tries to comprehend this astoundingly complex, refined art form often feels he is studying fleeting shadows. Initially, the wise foreigner does not attempt to understand wayang. *Instead, he examines the role of the* wayang, *and the* dalang, *in modern Javanese society.*

"A dalang's *duty is to inform, to instruct, and to entertain," says Ki Timbul, a leading dalang who was the subject of a recent documentary film for American public television.*

Thus, wayang *is widely used to disseminate information about government programs. The puppet and people shows also play a role in the moral instruction of the younger generation. They help instill traditional Javanese values in the face of rapid industrialization.*

Wayang *is also being adapted to reflect the changing times. As modern urban audiences do not have the time to watch an entire all-night show, many* dalang *are experimenting with compressed versions, two to three hours long. Movies have also had an influence. Many audiences insist on back-to-back action scenes instead of drawn-out dialogues on philosophy.*

One change that has received mixed reactions is the replacement of the traditional blencong *with an electric light. Though the old coconut oil lamp in the shape of an eagle with spread wings had to be tended constantly during a performance, the flickering light made the shadows come alive. The brighter light cast by electric bulbs enable larger audiences to enjoy each performance, but has changed the atmosphere.*

Another controversial innovation has been the introduction of color. Gasman, a Yogyanese artist and wayang *carver, has promoted experimental performances in which two* dalang, *sitting on opposite sides of the screen, train colored spotlights on the screen to add tone to the shadows — to mixed reviews.*

Back of the Book

This section provides a handy, compact package of exciting insights, entertaining tidbits and invaluable travel tips that will help enhance your trip to Yogyakarta and its environs. The main maps depict Yogyakarta and Central Java's most significant sites and features. Little-known facts about the city from the joys of scorpion oil extract to the wonders of Superman's lair are revealed in Yogya Trivia. The section on Tours includes detailed directions for taking a walking tour and *becak* tour of the city to an educational study of the Borobudur that will make your visit to the stupa that much more rewarding. The itineraries are accompanied by numbered maps that will help you get around on your own. Off the Beaten Track takes you further afield from Yogyakarta — to some of the most breathtaking terrain and stunning places of interest in the world. Best Bets is a digest of the best of everything that can be found in Yogya from the most intriguing place to hang out at midnight to the best batik boutiques. Finally, the Travel Notes summarize the essential basic information needed to get you to Yogyakarta and back home again — if you can bring yourself to leave.

The Tugu monument (left) stands at the crossroads of old and new Yogyakarta. To the south is Jl Malioboro and the kraton, to the east lies the modern shopping district along Jl Sudirman. Preceding pages: Tourist hordes at Borobudur.

Yogyakarta Trivia

FIGHTS BETWEEN TIGERS AND BUFFALOES were a favorite royal spectacle of the 18th century. As usual in Java the contests were imbued with deep symbolic meaning. The tiger represented the foreigners: it was quick and vicious but had little endurance. The buffalo by contrast was the stolid, plodding, patient Javanese. Needless to say, the buffalo always won.

EXQUISITE HAND-CRAFTED BATIK sometimes takes months to produce. Thus it is quite costly. It was worn mainly by the aristocracy because the common Javanese couldn't afford it. Eventually, many styles of batik became identified with one's social status. One design, the Parang Rusak or Broken Blade, was the exclusive privilege of royalty. President Reagan was given a Parang Rusak-style shirt during his state visit to Indonesia in 1986. No one is sure if it was a subtle Javanese comment.

DISGRUNTLED SUPPLICANTS would sit between the sacred banyan trees in the Alun-alun, in the Sultan's direct line of sight as he sat on his throne during the 18th and 19th centuries. Generally, the Sultan would see the supplicant and summon him to hear his complaint. For the audience, the supplicant would dress completely in white, representing purity. White is also the Islamic color of death, which the supplicant risked if the Sultan decided his complaint was frivolous and a waste of his royal time.

PALACE OF HIGHER EDUCATION. During the revolution. the front pavilions of the *Kraton* were used as lecture halls by the new Gajah Mada University. The medical school remained in the *kraton* until 1973.

SCORPION OIL EXTRACT is sold by one enterprising hawker on Jalan Malioboro as a skin tonic. He markets his product using live scorpions; he lets them crawl over his bare arms. Although the tonic may not prove to be effective, the scorpions themselves are; one sting and your case of acne suddenly becomes the least of your worries.

SUPERMAN'S restaurant in Pasar Kembang earned its name because the backpacker clientele of owner Pak Suparman mispronounced his name for a decade. He has officially changed the name of his eatery to Superman's to the delight of a new generation of young travelers. Now relocated in more spacious premises down the lane, Superman's still serves the best Western breakfast in town. According to local pundits, one hapless American missed out on his poached eggs and papaya juice; he had got the name of the place wrong — and spent two fruitless days searching for Spiderman's.

YOGYA COWBOYS. Like their cousins, the small, smiley gigolos of Kuta Beach in Bali, the young trendies of Yogyakarta are a permanent part of the furnishings in cafes along Jalan Malioboro. They keep their eyes peeled for young female Westerners to spend a few days with.

CRUISING THE COUNTRYSIDE on old motorcycles is a popular means of recreation on lazy Sunday afternoons in Central Java. Far from being Hell's Angels though, the Yogyanese bikers are generally older gentlemen riding BMW 250s. The bike's single cylinder produces a slow, steady rhythm reminiscent of a gamelan orchestra.

JUMA'AT KLIWON occurs every 35 days. The conjunction of Hari Juma'at (Friday) in the seven-day Islamic calendar and Hari Kliwon on the five-day Javanese calendar is considered especially holy. On Malam Juma'at Kliwon, the evening of the conjunction, large groups of mystics meditate in Parangtritis, hoping to communicate with Loro Kidul to increase their spiritual powers.

MYSTIC SYMBOLISM isn't only contained in the *kraton's* wood and stone carvings. The structure itself has mystical meaning. The nine gates of the complex represent the nine corporeal openings in human beings. The Hindu concepts of the male lingam and female yoni are symbolized by the phallic Tugu monument two kilometers to the north, and the Krapyak palace the same distance south. The *kraton* represents humanity, the union of the two.

MOUNT MERAPI is so volatile that six manned volcanology station's continually monitor the mountain's activity. Frequent lava and mud flows damage buildings and crops on the slopes. And offerings of food and clothing are regularly thrown into the crater to appease the volcano's spirits.

A COMPLETE EUROPEAN ORCHESTRA was maintained by Sultan Hamengkubuono VII for his amusement. For a brief period in 1928, before he went to Bali, the German composer and painter Walter Spies was resident conductor.

SIX HOURS IN YOGYA is the title of a classic film made by Indonesia's pioneer director Usmar Ismail. It tells the story of the Indonesian army's brief recapture of Yogyakarta from the Dutch in 1948. Today, *Six Hours in Yogya* not only describes one of the nation's finest hours. The phrase also sardonically refers to those tourists, predominantly Japanese, who fly into Yogya in the morning, breakfast at a local hotel, and charge madly about the countryside for six hours or so, briefly descending on venerable palaces and temples in camera-clicking frenzy, before they jet back to Bali.

LORO JONGGRANG means "slender virgin." It is named after a princess wooed by an unwanted suitor. Wishing to be rid of the man, she promised to marry him if he built an entire temple in one night. Using supernatural powers, he set about the task. Seeing that the gentleman was just about to complete the job, the princess ordered her servants

to start pounding rice. That in turn fooled the cocks into crowing prematurely to announce the dawn. Broken-hearted, the suitor gave up his quest. When he discovered he had been fooled, he turned the princess into stone. She remains in that stiff condition today in the northern chamber of the monument as Durga, consort to Siva.

THE SOLID TEAK PILLARS that support the Golden Pavilion in the *kraton* are, in the best tradition of Javanese syncretism, carved with the motifs of Java's three major religions. They are a golden Buddhist lotus leaf, a red Hindu motif, and the opening words of the Koran: "There is but one God," in highly-stylized black and gold Arabic script. According to one aged retainer, the pillars' motif symbolize the Javanese state being soundly supported by the peaceful coexistence of these three religions.

TAKE IT, IT'S ALL YOURS. When the hapless Pakubuono II lay dying in December, 1749, he summoned Dutch Governor von Hohendorff of the northeast coast, his only friend, and made him a remarkable proposition. Wishing to relieve himself of the burdens of state, he wanted to give the entire kingdom of Mataram to the Dutch. Taken aback, von Hohendorff tried to dissuade the susuhunan, but finally agreed to sign a document — which he wisely ignored. A few days later, von Hohendorff installed the Crown Prince as Pakubuono III.

FIRST FLIGHT. In June, 1946, the nascent Indonesian Air Force conducted the first test flights of the Zogling (German for "fledgling"), a pilot training

glider designed and built by Wiweko Supono and Nurtanio Pringgoadisuryo. Pulled by a Harley-Davidson motorcycle, the Zogling skewed and nosedived on the first two attempts as the pilot trainees tried to exert too much control over the craft. The third trainee, Hassan Purbo, reasoned that because the Zogling was designed to fly whereas he was not, Hassan simply held the stick steady as the craft was towed along the runway. The Zogling soared into the sky.

LAST LAUGH OF SULTAN AGUNG. During the disastrous siege of Batavia by Sultan Agung, the Dutch Commander, Jan Pieterszoon Coen, died of cholera and was buried in the city. Thirty years later, when his remains were to be moved to a newly-constructed church, the grave proved to be empty. According to legend, the Javanese spirited Coen's remains away soon after Sultan Agung's death in 1646, and buried his head under the steps leading to Agung's hilltop grave at Imogiri. Each pilgrim visiting Agung's mausoleum thus had to tread on Coen's skull, an action the Javanese consider a grave insult.

WHAT'S IN A NAME? A lot, if you happen to be a member of Yogyanese royalty. The royal name Hamengkubuono means "the world on his Lap." His subsidiary prince, Paku Alam, is "the axis of the universe." Yogyakarta's full Javanese name is Ngajogjakarta, which derives from Ayodhya, a capital in the Ramayana epic. Although most Yogyanese pronounce their city's name "Jogjakarta" as it used to be spelled, Indonesian television announcers currently pronounce it the way it's spelled, Yogyakarta. However, the commonly-used short form Yogya is always pronounced "Jogja".

WHAT'S NOT IN A NAME. Tourist legend states that Jalan Malioboro was named after the British Duke of Marlborough. But it seems unlikely the Yogyanese would name an important street after a European. According to most sources, Malioboro actually derives from a Sanskrit term meaning "garland-bearing street," a reference to the custom of strewing flowers on the roadway when the sultan passed. Many guidebooks also claim that the name Borobudur comes from the Sanskrit phrase *vihara Buddah uhr* — "Buddhist monastery on a high place." Actually it is an acronym for a more resounding phrase meaning: "Mountain of Accumulation of merits of the ten states of Boddhisatva."

WHEN DISASTER STRIKES Yogyakarta, court attendants carry the royal *pusaka*, the holy heirlooms, in a ceremonial procession around the Alun-alun. In another measure aimed at warding off catastrophe, officials walk around the outer *kraton* perimeter — a distance of four kilometers — in a silent, nightlong vigil.

Yogya Tours

WALKING TOUR. Start your stroll at Yogyakarta's colorful bird market, **Pasar Ngasem (1)**, named for the area of the *kraton* where it is located. Any *becak* driver can drop you off there.

In Pasar Ngasem, there are hundreds of turtle-doves for sale, among dozens of other varieties of fowl. A few of the turtle-doves, costing as little as Rp 2-3000, might be destined for the dizzying heights of national or international dove singing competition after they undergo extensive training (see Heavenly Songs in the Wind).

You will also find a fascinating assortment of bird life from all over the vast Indonesian archipelago. International transport of these birds is prohibited, however, so look but don't buy unless you plan to live in Indonesia.

The tumbledown arches of **Taman Sari (2)** serve as a brooding backdrop to Pasar Ngasem. (**See inset map 1 for guide through Taman Sari**). From the main entrance of the bird market, make your way past rows of low tables and straw mats laden with a vast array of vegetables, spices, and live fish to the back of the market. Turn right, then left again. You should arrive at an alleyway called KPIII, and be directly in front of **Sunarya's Batik Painting Studio (3)**.

Turn right again, then left at a staircase leading to the **Kenogo (A)**, the large palace within Taman Sari that was once in the center of the Serangan pool. Walk through the Kenogo to the south entrance and turn right. A few meters along, on your left, is the entrance to the underground passageway (B) which originally led underwater to the other part of Taman Sari. Passing this, further along, is **Sumur Gemuling (C)**, a circular well believed to have been the mystic center of Taman Sari.

From Sumur Gemuling you have two options. If you wish, you can retrace your steps to the underground passageway, descend the stairs, and walk through to the far entrance. You will emerge on a **platform (D)**, where someone's laundry is usually drying behind you. Walk out to the road, then turn right and continue to the main entrance to the **Umbul Binangun (E)**, the Sultan's Bathing Pools. From Sumur Gemuling, you can also head south, through the kampung, to the **Gedung Gapura Agung (F)**, the sultan's meditation platform. The west wall, elaborately decorated with arborial designs, has been restored. The Umbul Binangun will be behind the high wall opposite the Gedung Gapura Agung. The gate is generally closed, so you will have to walk around, through the kampung, and approach the main entrance from the south.

The bathing pools have been largely restored, complete with boys diving for coins. These pools were the heart of Taman Sari, where the sultan would pass the scorching hot afternoons relaxing on water-cooled couches. The **three-story tower (G)** standing between the two larger pools and the smaller private pool to the south is where the sultan would watch his concubines frolic in the water.

Returning to the main entrance to the pools, walk 100 meters to the east to Jalan Taman, then left again, following the high walled street to Jalan Ngasem. From there you can retrace your steps up that street to the first right turn onto Jalan Rotowijayan. Or you can cut through the alleyways of the **outer kraton kampung (4)**. This neighborhood is reserved for families with some connection to the sultan, either relatives, some quite distant, or kraton servants and other employees.

By whichever route, and after running a gauntlet of souvenir sellers and becak drivers, you will arrive at the east entrance to the **inner kraton (H)**. (**See Inset Map 2 for details of Kraton**.) Passing through the East gate, you enter the **Kemandungan Utara — Keben Courtyard (I)**. The **Ponconiti Pavilion (J)** in the center is now the territory of beggars and tacky souvenir sellers. Here you pay a tiny entrance fee and acquire an aged retainer in full traditional costume as your guide.

From the Keben Courtyard you pass through the **Srimaganti Gate (K)** to a courtyard with two pavilions containing some of the courtly paraphernalia called *pusaka*. The **Srimaganti Pavilion (L)** to the right houses two *gamelan* orchestras. Nagawilaga, tuned to the scale of *slendro*, is said to be two hundred years old, and the other, Gunturmadu is tuned to the *pelog* scale and reputed to be over half a millennium old. These *gamelan* are taken to the Grand Mosque once a year and played during celebrations of the Prophet Muhammad's birthday.

In the **Trajumas pavilion (M)** opposite are palanquins for weddings, litters, and chairs. A huge rattan cage, which resembles a large-scale version of the cage used to keep fighting cocks, was where each of the sultan's children were placed when they reached seven months, the age in which they were first permitted to touch the ground. Various toys were placed in the cage. The first toy the infant picked up was said to determine his future character.

At the far end to the south are two huge, stone statues of *raksasa* — giants — flanking the **Donopertopo Gateway (N)** into the central courtyard. The *raksasa* appear to be identical. However, the palace retainers say that the one to the left of the doorway, Cinkorobolo, has mainly a good nature. His companion, Bolouboto, is the bad guy. Although having the good giant on the left seems to contradict Javanese convention — in the wayang, the good, refined heroes are placed on the right of the screen. When viewed from behind, that is facing north towards Mt. Merapi, the statues are in the proper positions.

The entrance guarded by the *raksasa* leads to the

central courtyard, **Plateran Kedaton (O)**. On the right is the centerpiece of the *kraton*, the **Bangsal Kencono (P)** or Golden Pavilion. Situated in front of the sultan's office and private living quarters, the Golden Pavilion was the venue for Wayang Wong and other cultural performances during the heady years of Javanese royal pomp and artistic splendor in the 1930's.

Standing in front of the Bangsal Kencono are three smaller pavilions: on the north a bandstand, where musicians played, as you can see from the European instruments wrought in stained glass along the eaves. Court attendants would wait in the other two pavilions.

The south gateway, **Kemanganang (Q)**, leads to private apartments and the pavilions facing the southern *alun-alun*. Incorporated into this gateway is the double naga snake with the name Dwinogor osotunggal, which gives the date of the *kraton's* founding Javanese year 1682 or AD 1756 — in reverse.

The sultan's private office, the **Gedung Purworetno (R)**, and the **Gedung Kuning (S)**, the sultan's living quarters, are immediately to the right of the Bangsal Kencono. Generally closed to the public, the Gedung Kuning is where the *pusaka* — the ceremonial kris, manuscripts, musical instruments and other sacred treasures — are safe-guarded.

Behind the Bangsal Kencono are the **Bangsal Proboyekso (T)** and the **Gedung Keputrian (U)** where the sultan's family lives. On the eastern side of the Plateran Kedaton is the **Kesatrian Gateway (V)**, which leads to the cultural wing of the *kraton*. The **Kesatrian Pavilion (W)** contains a *gamelan komplet*; on it, the court musicians can play all the songs in the Javanese repertoire. Every Sunday morning, the Kesatrian Pavilion gently reverberates to other worldly *gamelan* rhythms as the royal dance troupe, in full traditional dress, holds their weekly practice.

To the north, the **Gedung Kopo (X)** is filled with royal bric-a-brac. To the south, the **Royal Art Museum (Y)** has a collection of portraits of past sultans. Most were painted with indifferent artistic merit. A series of stylish black-and-white portraits on the other hand were painstakingly colored by hand. Also on display are charts of the royal family trees in which the male children are represented by fruit, females by leaves.

You can leave this part of the *kraton* by retracing your steps to the east entrance. Exit through the gate, then turn right and follow the road northward, keeping the *kraton* wall on your right. On your left is a small **museum (5)** that contains an impressive collection of 19th century royal coaches.

Continuing northward, you pass through the archway leading to the **Alun-Alun Lor (6)**, the north

LOCATION MAP

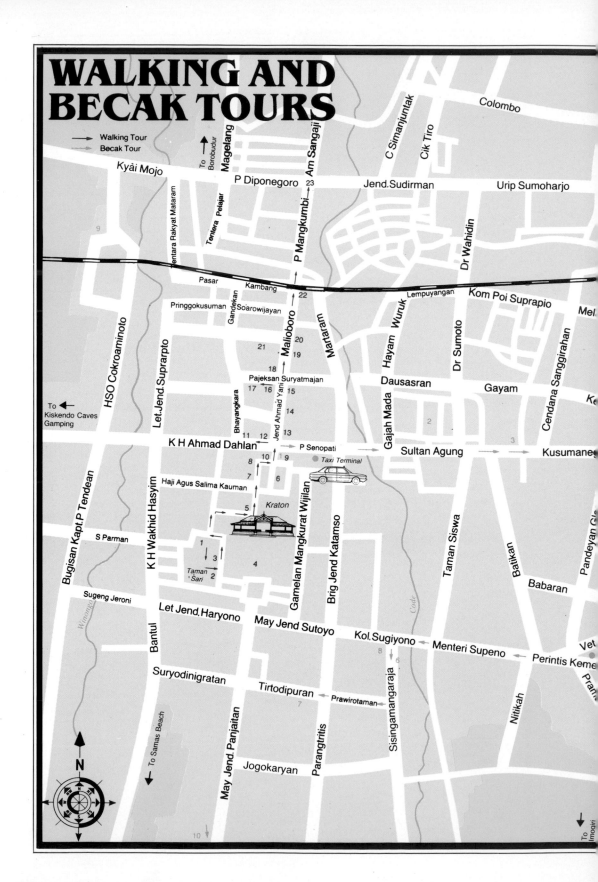

WALKING AND BECAK TOURS

→ Walking Tour
→ Becak Tour

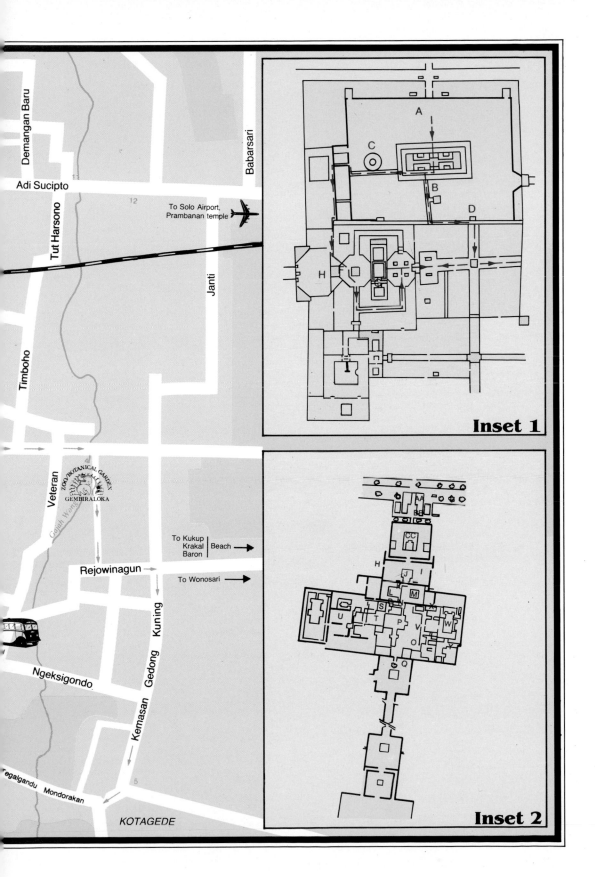

Demangan Baru

Adi Sucipto

Tut Harsono

Babarsari

To Solo Airport,
Prambanan temple

Janti

Timboho

A

C

B

D

H

Inset 1

Veteran

ZOO BOTANICAL GARDEN
GEMBIRALOKA

Gajah Wong

To Kukup
Krakal | Beach
Baron

Rejowinagun

To Wonosari

Ngeksigondo

Kemasan Gedong Kuning

Tegalgandu   Mondorakan

KOTAGEDE

AA

CC

H   I
J
L R M
C
L S
U T P V W
O
Q
Y

Inset 2

palace square. Turn right and cross a large terrace to the gateway to the **outer kraton pavilions (AA)**, where you pay another nominal entrance fee. During the revolution, these pavilions served as the first premises of Gajah Mada University. The medical faculty remained here until 1973.

Near the **Pangrawit Pavilion (BB)** is a scale model of the *kraton*. Other pavilions have displays of courtly life.

The staircase behind the pavilions leads to the **Siti Hinggi (CC)**, or high land, the main audience hall. This pavilion is now enclosed and has been made into a tableau depicting a typical 18th century audience with the sultan. Standing directly in line with the throne and looking north, you can see on a clear day the Tugu Monument at the far end of Jalan Mangkubumi, two kilometers distant. Beyond that stands the perfect cone of Mt. Merapi. The sultan used the view of the Tugu as an aid to meditation when he permitted audiences with his subjects. Even today, it is forbidden to place billboards along Jalan Malioboro which could obstruct the sultan's view.

Leaving the *kraton,* you cross the Alun-Alun Lor. This great ceremonial parade ground is now used mostly as a playing field for friendly soccer matches and for carnivals and performances. To your left is the **Grand Mosque (7)**, built in 1773. It is the focus of activity during Sekatan and other spectacular festivals.

The next stop on your walking tour is the **Sono Budoyo Museum (8)**. Opened in 1935 by the Java Institute, the Sono Budoyo has an extensive collection of prehistoric artifacts. The museum offers good examples and interesting explanations of the important Javanese crafts: wayang, kris, and batik. Particularly interesting are the carved wayang puppets representing Europeans. The museum also boasts an extensive Balinese art collection, including an entire Balinese temple in a back courtyard.

Leaving the Alun-Alun Lor, you embark on a two kilometer stroll up Yogyakarta's main street, Jalan Malioboro. Although the entire stretch is commonly called Malioboro, it technically changes names four times. The first stretch from the Alun-Alun is Jalan Trikora; it commemorates the military operation to liberate West Irian from Dutch control in 1963. At the first intersection, the name changes to Jalan A. Yani. For consistency's sake (or should we say inconsistency's sake), the cross street also changes name, from Jalan Senopati to Jalan Ahmad Dahlan. The two stolid edifices at the corner are the **Central Post Office (9)** on your right facing north, and the **Bank Dagang Negara (10)** on your left.

Cross the street. The first building on the other side is an **art's center (11)**. It used to be a favorite venue of Dutch society, back in the days when Jalan Malioboro was so well kept you could sit on the sidewalk in one's white cotton trousers without getting them dirty. The next building is the **Governor's residence (12)**, originally the Dutch Resident's house. During the revolution, the structure became the state palace. It is now used as a guesthouse for visiting dignitaries and other VIP's overnighting in Yogyakarta.

Across from the palace, **Fort Vredeburg (13)** has now been renovated as an historical museum. Although Vredeburg most likely is a corruption of the name of J.R. van der Burgh, the governor-general of Java's north coast during the early years of Yogyakarta, some say Vredeburg means "house of peace." If this is the case, you can view the "peacemaker," the fort's only cannon emplacement, which is aimed south right at the *kraton.*

North of the fort is **Pasar Beringharjo (14)**, Yogyakarta's main market. This is a typical Javanese market reeking with pungent smells and rife with piquant — and sometimes offputting — sights. In the cavernous interior which resembles a Middle Eastern bazaar, hundreds of stalls sell meat and fish, fruit stacked in tall pyramids, bolts of batik and other textiles, household goods and an extensive collection of bamboo and rattan handicrafts.

Beyond the market's entrance is a row of shops. They culminate in **Terang Bulan (15)**, Yogyakarta's premier batik store. The prices are fixed but the quality is guaranteed.

Across the street, the **Mirota (16)** is Yogyakarta's original Western goods supermarket. It has branches all over town. The next stop, across the street from the **New Happy Restaurant (17)** (good fried vegetables) is a **Chinese medicine shop (18)**, which sells a vast array of traditional Chinese medicines and Javanese herbal medicines called *jamu.*

The **Tourist Information Office (19)** across the street is well worth a visit if you heed the notice outside. The illustration of a young Western couple outfitted in early 70s hippy clothing is a hint that you should be properly dressed before entering.

Along this section of Malioboro is the **Mutiara Hotel (20)** and several tourist-oriented restaurants. Most serve mainly Indonesian-Chinese meals. Several souvenir and textile shops also line this route. To the left is the **Chinese market. (21)**

On reaching Jalan Sosrowijayan, Malioboro continues onward past the historic **Hotel Garuda (22)** and the railway tracks, where it changes name again to Jalan Mangkubumi, for another few hundred meters to the **Tugu Monument (23)** where it ends.

You, however, can turn left into Sosro, or Pasar Kembang, the warren of small homestays and restaurants, several of which now serve passable pseudo-western food at extremely low prices.

Becak Tour

A *becak* tour is usually the highlight of a visit to Yogyakarta. The relaxed pace of the open pedicab is far more appropriate to enjoying the city's special atmosphere than an automobile or bus. The southern part of the city, where the attractions are too far apart to walk, is particularly rewarding *becak* tour country.

You can hire your *becak* outside of most hotels. The wiry men and boys who drive them for a living gather out front to compete for passengers everyday. Another convenient starting point would be in front of the **Central Post Office (1)**.

On the standard tour covered by most drivers, the first stop is usually Yogyakarta's other *kraton,* the palace of the subsidiary **Paku Alam royal house (2)**. This palace, established in 1813 by Raffles for his aid in storming the main *kraton,* is now open daily. The buildings and royal paraphernalia are similar to the main *kraton,* though on a less lavish scale.

The **Batik Research Center (3)** on Jalan Kusumanegara is the headquarters of Yogyakarta's batik industry. You can get information there about prices, quality, and batik courses.

The next stop on the standard route is the **Gembira Loka Zoo (4)**. Though nowhere near as big as the zoos of Jakarta or Surabaya, Gembira Loka is a pleasant place to spend an hour or so, except on Sundays or holidays when it's jam packed with people. The main attraction is two Komodo dragons, the giant carnivorous monitor lizards that inhabit only Komodo Island and a few surrounding landfalls east of Bali.

Next you will be treated to a long bumpy ride down Jalan Veteran during which the muscle power of your driver's legs will amaze you. Your destination is **Kota Gede (5)**, the site of Senopati's *kraton.*

Kota Gede is a rather uninteresting village. But it has some 19th century architecture, Senopati's gravesite, and scores of silverworking shops producing some of the finest inexpensive to mid-price jewelry in Indonesia.

Senopati's tomb is open only on Monday mornings and Friday afternoons. The most interesting time to visit is after 8 pm on Thursday when crowds of Javanese pray outside the gates of the graveyard in the belief they get mystic power from Senopati and the 80-odd other members of Yogyakarta's nobility buried there. A duct system carries the rainwater that has washed over the tombs to holding ponds, where pilgrims fill containers with the water they use as a panacea.

Peddling back along the southern road, the driver's next stop is likely to be the **Independence Struggle Museum (6)** on Jalan Sugiyono, if it's still before 12:30. This museum contains a small collection of photographs of the Indonesian struggle for independence from the Dutch.

The last stop on the tour is the batik factory area in **Jalan Tirtodipuran (7)**. When the *kraton* ceased to be the major source of batik earlier this century, the center of Yogyakarta batik production moved south of the *kraton* walls to this area. Many homes and small-scale factories here produced batik *cap* cloth and ready-made garments, and some batik **tulis**. All factories will demonstrate the batik-making process. Bear in mind that your driver may receive a well-deserved commission from any shop he takes you to where you purchase something.

If you start your *becak* tour before 8 am, you should arrive in Jalan Tirtodipuran in time for lunch at one of the tourist-oriented restaurants in the area. Many atmospheric but inexpensive restaurants have sprung up in the area to augment the streets' burgeoning guest house clientele. It will also get you back before the relentless afternoon sun begins taking its toll on tourist and *becak* drivers alike.

If you have some time left and your driver still has the energy, ask him to take you to the restored house of the Indonesian army's first general, Sudirman, near Prawirotaman on **Bintaran (8)**. It has been turned into a small museum of his life and his role as ranking general during the revolutionary war of independence.

There are several other interesting locations on the outskirts of Yogyakarta that are accessible by *becak*. But make sure you confirm the agreed price beforehand for any side trips.

One worthwhile stop is the house where the 19th century aristocratic rebel Diponegoro lived, four kilometers out of town in **Tegalrejo (9)**. The buildings, which were burned down by the Dutch in 1825, were rebuilt in 1969. Just two kilometers due south of the *kraton,* in the village of **Krapyak (10)**, is a two story-brick building known as Adukidang that may have been a hunting lodge. Mangkubumi retired here in 1791 before he died. The building is an architecturally-impressive structure.

On the road to Solo near the Hotel Amburrukmo is the kitchy architecture of **Affandi's private art museum (11)**. Affandi, now in his eighties and in declining health, is universally considered Indonesia's leading modern artist. Though some critics consider his brand of neoexpressionism the work of a superannuated finger painter, many of Affandi's huge canvases explode with undeniable power and vitality. The museum also features work by Affandi's talented daughter Kartika and other young Yogyakarta artists.

Farther along Jalan Solo is the sadly-neglected **Handicrafts Center (12)**. Though underutilized, it's worth a visit just to see the wide range of Indonesian Handicrafts on display.

Temple Tour

Borobudur (1) is one of the most impressive man-made monuments on earth. Located just 45 kilometers northwest of Yogyakarta, it's a short trip by hired car or public bus that can be covered in one morning. But give yourself ample time to explore the monument itself. Once you get there, you will probably be mesmerized into lingering for hours like most other visitors except, of course, the jet-setting Japanese.

Borobodur takes the shape of a stupa, the characteristic Hindu temple representing the holy Mt. Meru. It was built near the confluence of the Progo and Elo Rivers, which are also believed to correspond to the confluence of the Ganges and Jumna in India.

Viewed from above, Borobudur takes the shape of a mandala, a visual aid to meditation. It is divided vertically into three sections: a square base that's now hidden, a series of galleries that encircle the lower levels, and the topmost terraces with their smaller bell-shaped stupas that enclose statues of the seated Buddha.

As part of the U.S.$60 million restoration of the monument, a grand, landscaped new walkway graces the Borobudur although it's a long, 1,500-meter climb to the monument's base. The tawdry collection of souvenir stands that once marred the gateway have now been thankfully relocated to the less obtrusive parking areas.

Begin your tour of Borobudur right at the base of Borobudur, where scenes depicting the world of earthly pleasures and the damnations of the afterworld are carved. Here, one section of the hidden foot has been uncovered.

The main section — a processional terrace and the five galleries — forms the pilgrims route to the top. A phenomenal 1,500 pictorial relief panels and another 1,212 ornamental pieces relate the Buddha's life story, his teachings, and deeds of the Bodhisattva. Circle through the galleries examining each for an enthralling glimpse of daily life in 9th century Java.

Then continue your climb to the top. The next levels above the relief panels contain 432 niches. Each, except for those that have been vandalized over the centuries, has a statue of Buddha displaying one of five hand positions or mudras; each symbolizing a different teaching.

A pilgrim, or traveler walking the complete route — always clockwise — will circle the monument nine times — and cover five kilometers.

Just as the carved panels at the base of the monument symbolize the world of flesh and desire, and the galleries the path toward enlightenment, the open spaces and simple forms of the upper circular terraces represent the renunciation of earthly constraints. Each of the 72 dagobs — the miniature stupas — once contained a statue of a

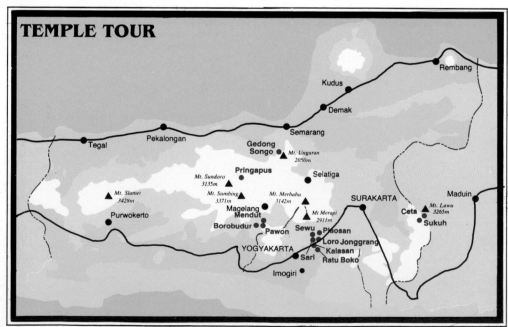

TEMPLE TOUR

meditating Buddha. Many were stolen or damaged during the years and have not been replaced or fully-restored. The pattern of light and shade created by the open latticework of the dagobs hall hides each statue in shadow. Pilgrims reach through the lattice to touch the Buddha statues for luck.

The topmost level is austere; the enormous empty stupa represents nirvana.

The Borobudur was probably built in three stages. The first and third stage appear to be the work of Hindus. The second major stage has the mark of Mahayana Buddhists. Still the monument as a whole shows a remarkable cohesiveness. Each relief contributes to the meaning of the whole.

Borobudur is actually the most conspicuous part of a complex of three temples. Nearby is **Candi Pawon (2)**, also called the "porch" or "kitchen" temple. Little is known about this temple, except that it was obviously the last stop on the pilgrim trail to Borobudur. A dwarf over the doorway pours riches from his bag.

Further back along the road to Borobudur from Muntilan lies **Candi Mendut (3)**, one of Java's most beautiful temples. Unlike the rather heavily symbolic reliefs of its big brother, Mendut bas reliefs portray Jakarta's folktales and fables, and beautifully-carved panels of Bodhisattvas and Buddhist goddesses.

Inside are three huge statues. The centerpiece is a remarkable three-meter Buddha. It is flanked by the Bodhisattvas Vajrapani and Avalokitesvara, each 2.5 meters tall. Below the trio is the Wheel of Law smack between two deer, referring to the first sermon given by the Buddha at the Deer Park in Benares.

PRAMBANAN GROUP

The plain east of Yogyakarta is covered with ancient shrines and temples, both Buddhist and Hindu.

Head out from Yogyakarta along the road to Surakarta. For the first ruin of note, **Candi Simbasari**, turn left at a narrow, rough road leading to the village of Sambari 1.5 kilometers past the airport. This Hindu monument was only recently excavated. Because it was covered with ash for 500 years out of reach of vandals, thieves, and the weather, it is well preserved. The central lingga — the Hindu fertility symbol — is missing. But many smaller ones are scattered around the base.

The most famous and imposing temples of the Prambanan group are those of the **Loro Jonggrang** complex on the bank of the Opak River. These Sivaite temples were built by the Sanjaya dynasty soon after they took over Central Java from the Buddhist Sailendras. Arguably, they are the most beautiful and architecturally accomplished in Java.

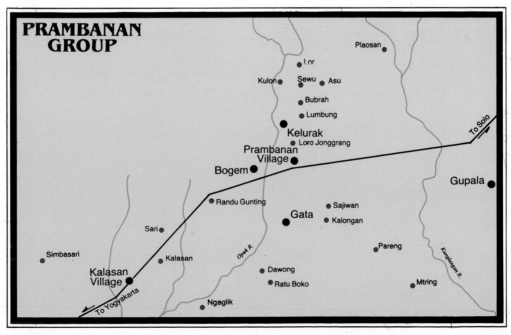

The reliefs of Loro Jonggrang display a wealth of sculptural detail. On the base are the Prambanan motifs — a zoo of sculptured animals. Above them are panels of celestial beings and scenes from the *Natyasastra,* the Indian dance manual. On the inner walls of the balustrade are reliefs depicting the *Ramayana* epic.

Facing Loro Jonggrang are the ruins of three temples which once contained statues of divine vehicles: transportation for the gods. Only Siva's celestial mount, Nandi the bull, has survived the centuries, however. He was once flanked by Hamsa, Brahma's gander, and Garuda, Vishnu's mythical eagle.

The other major groups of Prambanan are Buddhist temples built around the same time as Borobudur. From Loro Jonggrang, follow the road back, past rice fields for about two kilometers to Candi Sewi. This is actually a Buddhist monument built by the Hindu Sanjaya Kings, obviously as a sop to the religion of the majority of their subjects.

There are two other major Buddhist temples on the main Yogyakarta-Solo road. The first, **Candi Kalasan**, is located on the right side of the road just after the airport. No statues remain at this temple, but there is fine decoration on the outer niches.

The next, **Candi Sari**, is across the road from Candi Kalasan up a short track. This is an unusual two story building with six cellas. The upper story was probably connected to the lower floor by a wooden staircase at one time. This building is noted for its bas reliefs of female divinities and bodhisattvas playing musical instruments.

Two other major Buddhist temples lie behind Loro Jonggrang. Two kilometers along the narrow road leading past the Prambanan temple parking lot is **Candi Sewu**. The complex consists of 240 shrines arrayed around the main shrine guarded by huge stone *raksasa* armed with clubs.

Following the same road for another two kilometers will take you to **Candi Plaosan**. This has the same two-story construction as Candi Sari. Like Candi Mendut, the cella probably once held a huge metal Buddha flanked by stone Bodhisattvas, and other Buddha statues on the second story. Only the Bodhisattvas remain. Outside are 174 smaller constructions in concentric circles; they are gifts from officials whose names are inscribed on the northwest corner of the first row of shrines.

The third major ruin group of the plain is **Ratu Boko**. To get to it, go to Prambanan, then turn south at the signpost "Yogyakarta 18 km" toward Piyungan. After about two kilometers, a small signpost points you to a steep path leading to the ruins.

Despite the name of the ruins — "King Boko's Palace" — the complex was probably also religious in nature. The first structures you see are a ceremonial porch and the foundations of two buildings. Turn south, then east. Passing through a village, you come to the major set of ruins: foundations, walls, and a set of bathing pools.

Early morning mists *cloak the Javanese landscape. In the fields, pools of water, re-flecting the early morning light, reveal* sawah *or wet rice cultivation. Flushed with rice Java is the granary of Indonesia.*

Off the Beaten Track

CLIMB FIRE MOUNTAIN, the classically cone-shaped volcano that forms an ominous backdrop for Yogyakarta. On a clear day, Gunung Merapi as it's called in Indonesian, is an active volcano and an important venue for Javanese mystic practices. The 2,911-meter peak is a difficult but possible one-day climb. Kaliurang, 25 kilometers from Yogyakarta and 900 meters in altitude, is a hill resort and the last village on the slopes. It has old Dutch hill station villas, a couple of swimming pools, and some interesting walks in the bush for those unwilling to tackle the climb to the crater.

Vogel's *losmen,* across from the children's playground in Kaliurang, is the local tourist information center where you can get information on the various routes to the summit. But most people actually climb Gunung Merapi from the shorter, less strenuous route that begins in Selo on the other side of the mountain. The Kaliurang route can take up to 15 hours for the round trip.

ONE OF THE MOST SACRED SPOTS IN JAVA, the royal tombs of Imogiri, is located only 15 kilometers south of Yogyakarta. To reach the tombs, head south from Kota Gede, or turn left at the sign on the Parangtritis road. The village of Parangtritis on Java's rugged south coast can also be reached directly from Imogiri; in fact, you must travel there by way of Imogiri if the bridge over the Opak River is closed.

The tombs are at the top of a long staircase, a steep climb of 345 steps. They are open only on Mondays from 9 a.m. to 1 and on Friday afternoons from noon to 4 p.m.

The site consists of three major sections: the central tomb is venerated as the final resting place of Sultan Agung himself; it is flanked on the left by the tomb of the susuhanan of Surakarta and the sultans of Yogyakarta on the right. On Fridays, scores of pilgrims in traditional Javanese attire climb the steps to pray and engage in other mystic practices.

DARE TO ENTER THE LAIR OF THE LADY OF THE SOUTH SEAS, located in the rough seas off Parangtritis, 26 kilometers south of Yogyakarta. Parangtritis is ballyhooed as Yogyakarta's beach resort. But because of a combination of currents and the strange morphology of the seabed, the surf is utterly unsafe for swimming.

Legend has it that an amazon spirit soldier of Loro Kidul, the Queen of the South Seas, would bathe in these pools. She would entice any passing male to join her and the queen for a little sport and mating, then lure the hapless man to a watery grave.

Recent events lend some truth to the tale. Foreign visitors drown at Parangtritis regularly. There is even a story of dubious authenticity about an entire Japanese karate team that fell victim to the sea one by one. Each man jumped in the water to help a floundering team-mate, and was in turn caught in the crosscurrents.

The government plans to excavate an artificial bay for swimmers, which means the construction of big hotels and discos may not be far behind.

Meanwhile, Parangtritis is a place to relax quietly on the beach and perhaps wade along the shore, but not to go swimming or diving. Presently, it boasts a few basic *losmen* and equally basic *warung* serving fried noodles and rice. You can swim in the fresh water pools behind the village.

One spectacular event to look out for is the Labuhan festival, which takes place every six months. Because the sultan's hair and nail clippings retain some mystic power, they must be disposed of with proper ritual. During the Labuhan festival, they are carried from the *kraton* north to Mount Merapi, to the east and west, and, most elaborately, south to Parangtritis to be presented to the Queen of the Southern Sea. Dozens of retainers in full dress accompany the gilded box to the sea, where prayers are said. The offerings are thrown into the sea or buried in the sand, and flowers are sprinkled on the waves.

LOOK AT YOGYAKARTA's MIRROR IMAGE, the city of Surakarta, also known as Solo, 63 kilometers to the northeast. While each city boasts its own venerable *kraton,* lively arts scene and well-developed handicrafts trade, Solo is far more sedate and conservative.

Both the main *kraton* and subsidiary Mangkunegaran Palace are open to the public. The Pakubuono Kraton, now renovated after a disastrous fire in 1985, is essentially a carbon copy of Mangkubumi's *kraton* in Yogyakarta: open courtyards, inner pavilions, and a virtual city enclosed by massive walls. The nearby Mangkunegaran Palace, on the other hand, is similar to a Javanese home, though on a giant scale.

Solo is also a good shopping town. Several large batik factories produce much of Indonesia's exports. All have showrooms downtown. Pasar Klewer near the *kraton* is largely devoted to batik and other textiles. Pasar Triwindu is a flea market, with valuable antiques buried in huge piles of outright junk.

ASCEND TO THE HIGHEST INHABITED AREA IN JAVA, the Dieng Plateau. This misty, mystical region is also the site of the earliest Javanese temples. Dieng, which means "Abode of the Gods," was ruled by the Sanjaya dynasty after they were evicted from the Mataram heartland by the Sailendra's. They constructed several Hindu temples to complement the earlier ones. Dieng, chill and silent, is still an important place for meditation. The Semar Cave is considered the home of Semar,

the wayang character who is also Ismaja, the patron god of Java.

The crumbling remnants of ancient Hindu temples enhance the supernatural airs that hang over Dieng. The temple ruins litter the floor of a volcanic depression which is more than 2,100 meters above sea level. It is hermetically sealed off from the sobering realities of the rest of the island — and the world — by its altitude and an imposing mountain ridge.

Dieng may have had as many as 50 temples at one time; only eight have survived the ravages of time and volcanic activity in good enough condition to be restored. Their architecture is more austere than the elaborate temples of the better-known Prambanan group some 150-kilometers to the southeast.

Five temples are immediately visible from the popular southeastern entrance to the Dieng Plateau, clustered on a flat marshy plain. Centuries after they were built, four of them came to be named Arjuna, Srikandi, Puntadewa, and Sembadra, after characters in the epic Hindu poem, the Mahabharata. The fifth was named after Semar.

While his temple is readily accessible, his cave is set back in the woods behind Telaga Warna, the Colored Lake, and Telaga Pengilon, the Mirror Lake. Story has it that President Suharto himself regularly meditates in the cave.

The other two temples that have been restored at Dieng are Bima, up a hill and behind some trees along the road west of Semar's cave, and Gatutkaca. Bima sits atop the faces of what appear to be demons peering from portals. Steaming fissures in the earth and craters of bubbling, noxious-smelling, volcanic sludge up the road behind Bima provides a fittingly hellish backdrop. On the other hand, several crater lakes, flower gardens and the rolling pastoral vistas are simply heavenly.

It's possible to drive up from Yogya through gorgeous mountainsides of tobacco plantation in less than five hours, see all the sights, and get back by dark. But you can overnight on the plateau itself. Most accommodations there are quite primitive and fly-ridden, however. A better spot to break the journey is the clean, cool hill town of Wonosobo which has several hotels and *losmen*.

ENTER THE HOUSE where the 19th-century aristocratic rebel, Diponegoro, lived. Rumah Diponegoro is four kilometers out of town in Tegalrejo. The buildings which were burned down by the Dutch in 1825 were rebuilt in 1969. In addition to some paintings of Javanese history, the house also features the hole in the wall that Diponegoro supposedly made with his bare fists so he and his supporters could escape.

SEEK OUT KRAPYAK, a village where there is a two-story brick building known as Adukidang. Located two kilometers due south of the Kraton, the building may have been a hunting lodge. Its name is derived from *adu* which means contest and *kidang* which means deer. Mangkubumi retired in 1791, a year before he died at age 80. The building itself is an impressive structure with a vaulted central area opening on four sides.

Best Bets

MAMA'S GADO GADO. Mama has been a surrogate mother to lonely backpackers for years. She still serves her matchless *gado-gado* (vegetable salad) and *nasi campur* (a mixture of rice, vegetables, bean curd and more) in her restaurant on Jalan Pasar Kembang. Many Yogyanese eat there too: that's a sure sign of good quality and reasonable prices.

FRIED CHICKEN. Nyonya Suharti on Jalan Solo near the airport is renowned for serving the best *ayam goreng*, as fried chicken is called in these parts. As one American resident of Yogyakarta remarked, referring to the Kentucky Fried Chicken outlet down the road, "Nyonya Suharti has the Colonel plucked." The nyonya's style of fried chicken is called *Mbak Berek*.

TEH POCI. For romantic trysts, the Teh Poci cafe on Jalan Sudarso near the public swimming pool is ideal. Open from 7 p.m. to the wee hours, the dimly-lit bamboo establishment has rattan curtains that provide optimum privacy. As its name implies, the cafe specializes in Teh Poci, a strong tea poured into a small ceramic mug that contains about a quarter kilo of rock sugar. On request, you will get a table full of various traditional Yogyanese sweet snacks. Diabetics beware.

GUDEG WIJILAN is one of Yogyakarta's original *warung gudeg*, the nameless restaurant on Jalan Wijilan, near the east gate to the *kraton*, that features sweet *gudeg*, just as the Yogyanese like it. The restaurant's *gudeg*, made fresh daily, will last a week without refrigeration.

THE KOREAN GINSENG HOUSE is easily the best Korean restaurant in Yogyakarta; in fact, it's the only Korean restaurant in the city. It contributes to Yogyakarta's cosmopolitan atmosphere with a menu offering ginseng seaweed soup, bulgogi, and other dishes. Upstairs, the One and One Coffee house has live MOR music most nights.

THE CRAZY HORSE advertises itself as the best disco in ASEAN. Located in Borobudur Plaza on Jalan Kaliurang, the Crazy Horse is the hangout for local rich kids. The Rainbow in the Hotel Mutiara on Jalan Malioboro is another lively nightspot. The venerable and funky Ken Dedes has closed, but is scheduled to reopen in Parangtritis.

BECAK DRIVER. Disregard the mythical English-speaking Gajah Mada University student who is peddling his way through college. The best *becak* driver is probably Mugio, who hangs out in front of the Hotel Garuda. Mugio will take you anywhere in the city for Rp750 an hour.

ART GALLERY. Amri Yahya, one of Yogyakarta's leading artists, has a gallery and batik boutique on Jalan Gampingan, near the Fine Arts Academy (ASRI). Amri is primarily an abstract painter, but he also dabbles in purely decorative batik painting.

BATIK PAINTING. Among the marginally-talented practitioners of batik painting, Yogyakarta's controversial "traditional art form," Sunarya produces more than the standard "full moon over ricefields" style of trad-kitsch. His shop on KMPIII/120 A is right in front of Pasar Ngasem.

PLACE TO RELAX. After a day of heavy sightseeing, kick back for a while listening to the peaceful cooing of turtledoves at the Nitour Travel office on Jalan Ahmad Dahlan. For a small entrance fee you get tea, snacks and uninterrupted peace and quiet.

BAK PIA. For dessert or snack, a Yogyakarta specialty is *bak pia*, a sweet dumpling filled with bean paste. Bak Pia 55 on Jalan Bayangkari is a veritable institution. Bak Pia 75, just up the street, is a rip-off imitation. Or, according to others Bak Pia 75 is the real thing and Bak Pia 55 the second rate competitor. You be the judge.

ULTIMATE JAVANESE MEAL. For groups of at least 30, Hadinogoro's, the Sultan's brother, will serve an authentic royal Javanese meal at his palace. Vista Travel in the Hotel Garuda will make the arrangements.

PLACE TO HANG OUT AT MIDNIGHT. Both *Mbak Berek* fried chicken and *gudeg* are served on Jalan Malioboro from 9 p.m. until dawn. The Malioboro food stalls are unique in Indonesia — woven mats laid on the sidewalk. The more upmarket establishments provide low Japanese-style tables for your food. Malioboro after midnight is a favorite rendezvous for Yogyakarta's student and artist communities.

WAYANG PUPPET MAKER. The craftsman who makes puppets for Yogyakarta's master *dalang* is Pak Sagio. He runs a modest shop in Gendeng, a village 8 kilometers from Yogyakarta. Take the Jalan Bugisan road past Bagong's Pondok Pedepokan, then turn left at the banyan tree with the old woman selling tea underneath.

SILVERSMITH. The inventor of the model silver *becak* now seen in every souvenir shop, Salim Widarjo, now only does custom work in his shop in Kota Gede.

STAMPS. To keep track of borrowed books or other articles, stamp makers on Jalan Malioboro will produce a personalized impress in one day. These stamps feature characters from the wayang puppet theater and other inventive designs.

LEATHER GOODS. Yamin, a local leather craftsman, created the Yogya's first designer handbags by trimming used Dayak rattan carrying bags with high quality leather. Yamin now has a full range of bags, wallets, and suitcases at his shop in the Hotel Ambarrukmo.

Travel Notes

Land and People

Yogyakarta is a Special District of the Republic of Indonesia, a vast nation of 13,677 islands straddling the equator for more than 5,120 kilometers from east to west. Yogyakarta is located in the center of Java, the country's most important and densely-populated island, about 600 kilometers from the capital city, Jakarta. The majority of Yogyakarta's inhabitants are Javanese, but there are large communities of other ethnic groups from around the archipelago. Most of the people of Yogya, as it's called for short, are nominally Muslim.

How to Get There

By Air

Many major international airlines fly to Jakarta, and most regional carriers now have direct flights to Bali. Yogyakarta is halfway between these international gateways. The national airline, Garuda Indonesia, offers several flights daily to Yogya from Jakarta, Bali and other major cities in the island nation. Two other Indonesian carriers have turbo-prop services at cheaper rates: Merpati flies from Surabaya weekly on Saturday, and Bouraq flies daily from Jakarta via Bandung and from Banjarmasin in South Kalimantan.

By Rail

There are three air-conditioned overnight services from Jakarta. The Bima Express, with reclining seats and some sleepers, leaves from Kota Station at four in the afternoon; it arrives in Yogyakarta the next morning at the inconvenient hour of 1:30, continuing to Surabaya.

The other services depart from Gambir Station, near Jakarta's hotel district. The Senya Solo and Senya Yogya both have reclining seats in first class. They leave Gambir at 5:30 p.m. and 7:30 p.m. respectively and arrive in Yogyakarta in the early morning. The going is slow particularly along some stretches of track where switching can take hours. And there's nothing to look at to relieve the boredom unless the moon is full and bright and the night cloudless. Once outside of Jakarta, electricity in the rural areas is minimal.

A daytime alternative is the Fajar express, with some first class coaches, which departs Gambir at 6:20 a.m., arriving in Yogyakarta at 3:30 p.m. The trip can seem much faster than the night train because of the often spectacular scenery and fascinating tableaus of life in Java's countryside.

The Mutiara Selatan leaves Bandung at 5:30 p.m., arriving in Yogyakarta at 1:50 a.m. The same train leaves Surabaya for the return trip at 5:30, arriving in Yogyakarta at 11:30 p.m. The Bima Express also leaves Surabaya at 4:10 p.m., arriving in Yogyakarta at 9:10 p.m.

By Bus

Buses depart from Pulo Gadung Station in East Jakarta around 2 p.m. Buy your ticket from a reputable travel agent. Otherwise don't hand over any money until you see the vehicle, because standards vary widely. Some use contraptions that look like left over from a Demolition Derby held before World War II. Others companies offer deluxe buses with airline-style seats, videos and toilets which make the 10 hour trip more comfortable. Buses of the latter type depart at 5 p.m. from Denpasar in Bali. Java has a dense network of road transportation. You can get from one town to another cheaply and easily. But the comforts — and discomforts of the vehicles — can be dramatically different. From neighboring Surakarta, express mini-buses, called "travel colts" leave from offices on Jalan Yos Sudarso every half hour.

When to Go

The best time to visit Yogyakarta is during the dry season, from April to October. However, a wet season visit is only marginally less pleasant. Even during the heaviest rains, usually in January and February, most mornings are clear. The rains routinely begin in mid-afternoon and it drizzles into the evening. During both seasons the sun can be deceptively powerful, especially during an afternoon of ruin-tramping. So you need protection if your skin is unaccustomed to the tropics. Use sunblock or suntan lotion with a strong degree of shielding, at least during the early part of your visit. And bring it with you. The prices of imported suntan lotions are high in Indonesia.

Customs and Entry Rules

All travelers to Indonesia must possess passports valid for at least six months from the day of arrival and a return or through air ticket. Nationals from 28 countries including the U.S., Australia, New Zealand and most non-communist countries receive automatic tourist visa chops upon arrival. That permits them to stay in Indonesia for up to two months. Extensions are not permitted. However entry by air or sea through ports other than Jakarta, Surabaya, Bali, Medan, Manado, Biak, Ambon, Batam and Pekanbaru requires a valid visa prior to arrival.

A visa for a period of up to 30 days that can be extended for up to three months can be obtained overseas prior to arrival. A *surat jalan*, a police permit, may be required for travel in some remote areas (but not Yogyakarta or Central Java). A *surat jalan* can be obtained in Jakarta at Police Headquarters. (*Markas Besar Kepolisian Republik Indonesia,* Jalan Trunojoyo, Kebayoran Baru.)

A maximum of two liters of alcoholic beverages,

200 cigarettes, 50 cigars or 100 grams of tobacco and a reasonable amount of perfume for personal use may be brought into Indonesia exempt from duty. Camera equipment, typewriters, computers, radios, and automobiles may be brought in provided visitors leave with them, but they must be declared at customs. Pornography, television sets, radios and cassette recorders, printed matter in Chinese characters, and Chinese medicines are prohibited. Penalties for bringing in narcotics are very severe.

There are no restrictions on the import or export of foreign currencies and travelers cheques, but the import or export of more than Rp50,000 is illegal.

A-Z General Information on Yogyakarta

Airport
Yogyakarta's Adisucipto Airport is located 8 kilometers from the center of the city. Taxis are available from the desk outside the arrival hall. Because Adisucipto is a domestic airport, all immigration and customs, as well as duty free shops, are located in the gateway airports in Jakarta and Bali.

Andong
These seemingly antique horse and buggies are even older than some of Yogya's buses, but they are still in daily use in Yogyakarta. They are ideal for a shopping tour or romantic moonlight cruise down the quiet streets. A few andong are also available in Prambanan for transport to outlying temple sites.

Bargaining
Bargaining should not be regarded as a battle between buyer and seller: it's more of an expected form of social intercourse. There are only two occasions where bargaining is inappropriate: making very small purchases such as soap or mosquito coils, or shopping in a store clearly marked as having fixed prices. The first offer is generally twice to three times what the seller expects to receive. You should reply with half of what you are willing to pay. So smile and enjoy yourself and let the haggling begin!

Becak
The common man's transportation in Yogyakarta, the becak, is also the vehicle of choice for a leisurely tour of the city. These three-wheeled pedicabs are found virtually everywhere. The becak drivers on Jalan Malioboro already know the standard tourist itinerary (See Becak Tour). Ask at your hotel desk about the current standard rate, then bargain hard with your driver and make sure that both the route and rate are well understood before you climb aboard.

Bookstores
Travel guides and some other English language books are available at the Tourist Information Center, Jl Malioboro 16. The Garuda and Ambarrukmo Hotels have English language books and newspapers in their shopping arcades. Several stationary shops on Jalan Malioboro stock current magazines, and one sidewalk vendor sells cheap back issues of Time, Reader's Digest and the Asia edition of Travel & Leisure (Conde Nast's Traveler, which is more honest and thus more useful than T & L has yet to arrive, so bring your own copies). For Indonesian books, try Gunung Agung on the corner of Jalan Mangkubumi and Jalan Diponegoro.

Bicycles
You can rent Dutch-style one-speed bicycles in Pasar Kembang for less an American dollar a day. Because Yogyakarta is relatively flat, biking is a great way to cruise around town and the neighboring villages. There is a bicycle lane all the way to the Prambanan, but some of the backroads to other parts of the complex are rugged and unsuitable for bicycles.

Bus Services
Hot, crowded and fiendishly uncomfortable orange buses travel several circular routes around the city. Regular bus services leave from several terminals to outlying villages and monuments. The main terminal is in the southern part of the city on Jalan Supeno. To get to the Borobudur Temple, first take the bus to Magelang from the main terminal or the bus stop at the intersection of Jalan Diponegoro and Jalan Magelang. Then change to a minibus at Muntilan for Borobudur.

Buses also leave from the main terminal for Parangtritis. For Prambanan and Kaliurang, minibuses depart from the Jalan Simanjuntak terminal in the north.

Clothing
Although the Yogyanese are conservative, they nonetheless appreciate comfort. Any light, loose but sufficiently modest clothing is appropriate. Daytime wear should be 100 per cent cotton to absorb your perspiration in the humid climate. Leather sandals are okay; rubber thongs are for becak drivers. Shorts are considered unsuitable for women, and barely suitable for men. If you are visiting someone's home or office, trousers and a short or long-sleeved shirt are essential for men. Light, tropical, but chic dresses are okay for women.

However, neckties are virtually non-existent in Yogya. Formal dress for men consists of a long-sleeved batik shirt, slacks, shoes and socks. Several shops sell high fashion batik formal wear at reasonable prices.

Communications

The Central Post Office is located at the corner of Jalan Malioboro and Jalan Pasopati, near the Alun-Alun. Telexes and telegrams can be sent from the post office, but international calls must be made from the telephone office on Jalan Laksda Yos Sudarso 9. Long distance phone calls from hotel rooms must go through the operator and generally have a hefty surcharge. Telefax and other non-vocal communication is available on request.

Courses

Whether you stay in Yogyakarta for a few days or a year, you can learn any of several traditional art forms. Arguably the best environment for serious dance study is at Bagong Kussudiardja's studio complex in the ricefields at Pondok Padepokan. It offers long-term courses in classic and modern Javanese dance. Follow the signs from the south end of Jalan Bugisan or ask at Bagong's Gallery, Jl. Singosaren Utara 9. Dance and gamelan classes are also available at Dalem Pujokusuman, Jl. Brig. Jen. Katamso 70.

Learning the rudiments of batik-making only takes a few days. Many batik artists offer courses to foreigners, but the quality of their teaching can differ greatly. Information about courses and teachers is available at the Batik Research Center on Jl. Kusumanegara 2.

The most highly recommended course is taught by Tulus Warsito in his studio at Jalan Wates 31. For groups of 15 or more, the Taman Sari Batik Painters Cooperative will arrange an intensive seven-day course. For enquiries ask at Jalan KP III/120 A in Taman Sari, or the Galar Gallery, Jl. Parangtritis 7.

If you want to try your hand at *pedalangan,* the art of manipulating *wayang kulit* puppets, the Habiranda Dalang School has training sessions at 7 p.m. daily, except Thursday and Sunday.

Currency

The Indonesia unit of currency is the rupiah. The largest bill is Rp 10,000, currently worth about US$6. Often, only hotels, large stores and restaurants can change big bills, so it is wise to carry wads of Rp1000 and Rp 500 notes.

You can change money at the Bank Dagang Negara across from the Post Office on Jalan K. H. Dahlan. The Hotel Garuda has a money changer in the Shopping Arcade, as does the Ambarrukmo.

Electricity

Power is 220 volts at 50 Hz. Voltage can fluctuate and outages are fairly common is some areas. Major hotels generally have backup power, but don't expect more than a candle in most hotels and guesthouses.

Festivals

Most festivals in Yogyakarta take place around the *kraton.* The dates are determined by the Islamic Lunar Calendar, often in conjunction with the Javanese Calendar. The Tourist Information Office and most hotels will have a schedule of events.

Sekaten is held every year during the seven days prior to Mohammad's birthday. Two ancient *gamelan,* Kyai Nogowilogo and Kyai Gunturmadu, are carried from the *kraton* to the mosque, accompaplayed alternately mornings and evenings. In addition, large mountains of rice called *gunungan* are carried from the kraton to the mosque, accompanied by a retinue of hundreds of costumed palace guards. Sekaten is followed by Garebeg Mulud, the day after Mohammad's birthday, when the *gamelan* are returned to the palace.

Garebeg Besar is another Islamic festival where hundreds of goats, cows, and buffaloes are slaughtered and the meat distributed to the poor. As in Sekaten, mounds of rice are carried in great ceremony to the mosque.

Labuhan is Yogyakarta's great pre-Islamic festival, generally held twice a year. As the sultan's used clothing, hair and nail clippings have great power, they are offered to Loro Kidul, along with women's clothing, betel nut, and flowers. The main ceremony takes place at Parangkusomo near Parangtritis, due south of the Kraton, while other offerings are made simultaneously to the north on Mt. Merapi, and two points to the west and east.

Siraman is the ritual washing of the holy *pusaka.* The faithful believe that the power of the sultan resides in these items which include sacred spears, kris, banners and *gamelan.* The rinse water is considered to have great power; the Javanese drink it as a panacea.

Waicak is the big Buddhist ceremony celebrating the birth of the Buddha. It is held every May during the full moon. Pilgrims from all over Indonesia and the region flock to Borobudur to pray and inaugurate new monks. A striking nighttime candlelit procession makes the climax of this festival an extraordinary spectacle that Cecil B. de Mille would have appreciated.

Sedangsono is a yearly Christian pilgrimage that's also held in May. Thousands of pilgrims walk to Sendangsono, 32 kilometers northwest of Yogyakarta, to a cave that holds a statute of the Virgin Mary. The well water here is also considered holy.

Guides

Licensed guides are available through any travel agent. Freelance guides can range from professional touts in the pay of handicraft shops to seminary students wishing to practice their English. Use your own judgement.

Health

Observe common sense travel rules: drink only boiled water, peel fruit. Those are the first steps to keeping you healthy in Yogyakarta. If you do fall ill, there are adequate medical facilities.

The best-equipped general hospital is the Rumah Sakit Panti Rapih, Jl.Cik Ditiro 30, Tel. 2233. An English-speaking doctor is available at the Hotel Ambarrukmo, Jalan Solo, Tel. 88488.

Hotels

Yogyakarta has a room for everyone, from visiting heads of state to backpackers staggering off the third class train from Jakarta. Wherever you stay do a bit of bargaining. Ask for a discount. You may get one. Accommodations include the following:

Expensive

Ambarrukmo Palace Hotel (251 rooms), Jalan Laksda Adisucipto, Tel. 88488, Cable: HOTEL AMBAR, Tlx: 02511.
Hotel Garuda (120 rooms), Jl. Malioboro 72, Tel. 86353 Cable NAHOGA, Tlx: 25174.
Hotel Mutiara (140 Rooms), Jl. Malioboro 18, Tel. 5173, 4531, Cable: MUTIARA HOTEL, Tlx: 25155.
Puri Artha (59 rooms), Jl. Cendrawasi 9, Tel. 5934, Tlx: 25147.
Sahid Garden (114 rooms) Jl. Babarsari Tel. 87078, Cable: SAHID GARDEN Tlx: 25195.

Moderate

Arjuna Plaza (24 Rooms), Jl. Mangkubumi 48, Tel. 3063, Cable: ARJUNA PLAZA.
Batik Palace (24 rooms) Jl. Pasar Kembang 29, Tel. 2149, Cable: BAPAHOT.
Sri Maganti (46 rooms) Jl. Urip Sumohardjo 63, Tel. 2881, Cable: SRIMAGANTI.

Guesthouses

Several families around the *batik* factories on Jalan Tirtodipuran welcome guests. Rooms are basic but clean and comfortable, some with air-conditioning. Rates are generally lower than the hotels and often include a good breakfast. Among the better ones are:

Duta Guesthouse, (15 rooms) Jl. Prawirotaman 20, Tel: 5219.
Indraloka Homestay (40 Rooms) Jl. Cik Ditiro 14, Tel: 3614.

Cheap

Inexpensive *losmen* and hotels are clustered in Pasar Kembang, near the railway station. If you are really broke, sleeping for a few nights on a table in Mama's Warung is a time-honored Yogyakarta tradition. *Losmen* include:

Asia Africa Hotel, Jl. Pasar Kembang 25, Tel: 4489
Aziatic Hotel, Jl. Sosrowijayan 6.

Hours

Government offices are open from 8 a.m. to 2 p.m., and to 11:30 a.m. on Fridays. Banking hours are 8 a.m. to 3 p.m. weekdays, 8 a.m. to 11:30 a.m. Fridays and 8 a.m. to 1 p.m. Saturdays. Most money changers are open until late. The Tourist Information Office is open from 8 a.m. to 8 p.m. Most shops close at 2 p.m. for a siesta, reopening at 5 p.m. until about 9 p.m.

Language

Most of the people of Yogya speak Javanese in daily life. Not only is the language difficult to learn, but the language forms change depending on who you are addressing, so you can commit a grave social offense by using the wrong verb form. Luckily, almost everyone speaks the national language, Bahasa Indonesia, which is much easier. Make sure you try to learn a few important words and phrases.

Movies

Yogyanese moviegoers' tastes lean heavily towards action pictures with censored violent scenes, teenage romance and what passes for soft-core porn in Indonesia. Most hotels have good in-house videos.

Museums

Yogyakarta's museums are open from 8 a.m. to 1 p.m. weekdays, 8 a.m. to 11:30 a.m. Fridays, and from 8 a.m. to 12 p.m. on Saturdays. Closed Sunday. Among them:
The Sono Budoyo Museum on the north side of the *alun-alun* contains an impressive collection of traditional Javanese and Balinese arts. The **Kereta Museum** on Jalan Rotowijayan, near the tourist entrance to the *kraton,* has a fascinating collection of ornate 19th century coaches used by the sultan.

Like many of Indonesia's bigger cities, Yogyakarta has several military museums. The **Sasana Wiratama** is part of the Diponegoro monument in Tegalrejo. It has exhibits of early 19th century weapons used by the guerrilla fighters in the Java War. The **Perjuangan Museum** on Jalan Sugiyono has a small collection of photographs documenting the revolution. A much larger and more interesting collection is at the Army Museum on Jalan Sudirman. The **Air Force Museum** in Wonocatur, 10 kilometers from Yogyakarta, has replicas of aircraft used in the revolution. The house of General Sudirman on Jalan Bintaran is now a museum honoring modern Indonesia's first great military leader.

The **Biology Museum,** Jl. Sultan Agung 22, has an intriguing collection of stuffed animals and birds from the entire archipelago. Affandi's museum on Jalan Solo is a private establishment exhibiting the work of Affandi, his daughter Kartini, and young, promising artists.

Newspapers

Kedaulatan Rakyat, the local newspaper, has listings of current performances and other events but it's published only in Bahasa Indonesia. English language newspapers from Jakarta such as the *Jakarta Post* and *Indonesian Times* are also available. A few copies of *The International Herald Tribune* arrive in Yogyakarta every mid-afternoon.

Performances

Some sort of cultural event happens virtually every evening in Yogyakarta. Many are held especially for tourists, but most are for the Yogyanese people themselves.

Ramayana dance performances are held every Monday, Wednesday, and Friday at 8 p.m. at the Dalem Pujokusuman on Jalan Brig. Jen. Katamso. The Santi Budaya Group also presents Ramayana dancing nightly at 8 p.m. at the nearby THR recreation park on Jalan Katamso 45. The Arjuna Plaza Hotel, Jl. Mangkubumi 48, sways with dancing on Monday, Wednesday and Friday at 8 pm. On Thursday afternoon at 5 p.m. there's a tourist *wayang kulit* performance, and Friday afternoon a presentation of black magic. The Agasta Foundation on Jalan Gedongkiwa MD 3/236 also presents tourist *wayang kulit* by young *dalang* daily at 5 p.m., and *wayang golek* on Saturdays.

If you prefer authentic *wayang kulit,* a major performance occurs on the second Saturday of every month in the Sasono Hinggil pavilion south of the *kraton.* Radio Republic Indonesia broadcasts these performances; they begin at 8:30 and continue until dawn.

For sheer spectacle, nothing can rival the sensational scenes staged during the four nights of each full moon of the dry season (May through October). Hundreds of dancers and musicians reenact the *Ramayana* stories at an open amphitheater behind **Loro Jonggrang** temple. Tickets are available through travel agents or at the door. Arrive early. Bring a cushion as the benches are concrete.

Recommended Reading

Aside from a few travel guides, there are no English language books specifically about Yogyakarta. But any treatment of Javanese life and culture must deal mainly with the city and environs.

Ageless Borobudur by Bernet Kempers (Servire/Wassenaar 1976) is the standard work on the monument. *The Temples of Java* by Jacques Dumarcay (Oxford University Press 1986) is a readable treatise on the ancient Mataram and Majapahit period ruins. The translator, Michael Smithies, also wrote a comprehensive, slightly academic guidebook called *Yogyakarta* (Oxford University Press 1986).

To understand the role of religion in Javanese

life, read *The Religion of Java* by Clifford Geertz (University of Chicago Press, 1960) Most of his early research is still valid, though his rigid classification of Javanese into *santri* and *abangan* classes will raise the hackles of most educated Indonesians. Another minus is the book's language; it's convoluted in an apparent attempt to sound highbrow and learned but mostly sounds like pretentious gobbledygook. Niels Mulder's *Mysticism and Everyday Life in Contemporary Java* (Singapore University Press, 1978) investigates the *kebatinan* phenomenon.

Scores of academics have researched Javanese art and culture during the past thirty years, producing a wealth of material. There is no better introduction to the wayang than On *Thrones of Gold* by James R Brandon (Harvard University Press 1970). It includes three *wayang lakon* ably translated into colloquial English by Brandon and leading wayang expert Pandam Guritno.

Claire Holt in her *Art in Indonesia, Change and Continuity* (Cornell University Press 1967) remains, by default, the standard authority on Indonesian art. Holt wrote the book as a lark, including only the artists she liked. *Javanese Gamelan* by Jennifer Lindsay (Oxford University Press 1979) examines the complex and sophisticated music of the gamelan.

For history buffs, M. Ricklefs' *Jogjakarta Under Sultan Mangkubumi* (Oxford University Press 1974) is a detailed, insightful and eminently readable account of the founding of Yogyakarta. A good companion piece for all of Indonesia is Ricklefs' *A History of Modern Indonesia* (Macmillan 1981). For an account of the Revolutionary Struggles, try Anthony Reid's *Indonesian National Revolution 1945-1950* (Longman: Hawthorne 1974)

Fans of 19th century travel adventure accounts will enjoy Eliza Scidmore's *Java, Garden of the East,* (Oxford University Press 1984). It's a lively account of an indomitable American woman's travels that was originally published in 1899. A more sedate and comprehensive account of early 19th century Java appears in Thomas Stamford Raffles' legendary *History of Java* (Oxford University Press 1978).

The most accessible volumes of Indonesian literature are by Yogyakarta playwright and poet W.S. Rendra. Good translations of his work are *Ballads and Blues: Poems* (Oxford University Press 1974) and *The Struggle of the Naga Tribe.*

Security
Violent crime is extremely rare in Yogyakarta, but theft is highly likely unless proper precautions are taken. Keep jewelry in the hotel safe, your camera in its bag when not in use, and refrain from exhibiting large wads of currency. Any guide or driver hired from a travel agency or hotel should prove trustworthy.

Tapes
Several stores on Jalan Malioboro sell low-priced music cassette tapes. You can both stock up on western music for your walkman, and check out the selection of local traditional music on individual players with headphones. Unfortunately, the days of rampant pirating of cassettes has ended. The practice has been outlawed. So the popular compilation sets and best offers for which Indonesia was notorious have disappeared.

Taxis
Metered taxis do not exist, but hourly hire taxis are available from the Hotel Garuda, Lia Art Shop on Taman Garuda, the Airport, and the Municipal Taxi terminal on Jalan Senopati in front of the Central Post Office.

Time
Yogyakarta time is seven hours ahead of GMT. Besides the official Western Indonesia Time (WIB) you should also be aware of Jam Karet (Rubber Time); it means what it implies — that any event seldom happens exactly on schedule.

Tipping
Major hotels and restaurants include a 10 per cent service surcharge in the bill. Otherwise, small tips are appreciated but not obligatory.

Tourist Information Office
The Tourist Information Office on Jalan Malioboro can answer virtually any question from where to catch the bus for Borobudur to how to rent a house. It's open from 8 a.m. to 8 p.m. daily.

Tours
A score of local travel agents will arrange city tours, trips to temples, tickets and transportation to cultural events, airline tickets and private overland transportation to other destinations in Java or Bali. Among the most reliable are Indonesia's original agency NITOUR on Jalan A Dahlan 71, Tel: 3165, TLX: 25158 and Sri Rama Tour in the Hotel Ambarrukmo, Tel: 88488 Ext 710.

Vehicle Rental
Motorcyles and self-drive vehicles are available from several agents on Jalan Pasar Kembang. An international driver's licence is required, and extraordinary courage and alertness highly-recommended.

Water
Tap water is undrinkable. A good alternative is mineral water, available in several brands and on sale everywhere.

Index

Photo Credits

Jeremy Allan: 48, 58-59, 86

Michel Bikker: Cover, 30, 31, 35 (top), 39, 42-43, 45, 48, 65 (bottom), 68, 71 (bottom), 71 (right), 76 (left), 76 (right), 85 (left), 87

Rio Helmi: 2-3, 22, 51

Leonard Lueras: 24-25, 32-33, 36-37, 46, 47, 52-53, 66-67, 71 (left), 78, 79 (left), 79 (right), 84, 88, 89 (left), 89 (right), 90 (left), 90 (right), 91 (left), 91 (right), 92 (left), 92 (right), 92 (bottom), 93.

Kal Muller: 6-7, 10-11, 41 (top), 44, 51, 54, 55, 56, 57, 70, 85 (right)

Luca Invernizzi Tettoni: Endpapers, 4-5, 8, 9, 12, 13, 14, 15, 16-17, 26, 27, 28, 29, 34, 35 (bottom), 40, 41 (bottom), 62-63, 65 (top), 72, 73 (left), 73 (right), 77, 80 (left), 80 (bottom), 80 (right), 81, 82-83, 85 (bottom), 94-95.

Ivan Polunin: 61